Chantemesle

Chantemesle

Chantemesle

ROBIN FEDDEN

ELAND

First published by John Murray in 1964

This edition first published by Eland Publishing Limited
61 Exmouth Market, London EC1R 4QL in 2002

Copyright © Robin Fedden 1964

ISBN 978 0 907871 92 7

Some episodes from this book have
appeared in the pages of *The Cornhill*,
The London Magazine and *Twentieth Century*

Cover Image:
The Chateau of Louveciennes (oil on canvas)
by Josephine Bowes (1825-74) © The Bowes Museum,
Barnard Castle, County Durham, UK /
The Bridgeman Art Library

Text set in Great Britain by Antony Gray

To Katharine & Frances

☙ One

T HE FEEL of the air that moves through the house, stirring the curtains, is the feel of June. The doors are open, and whichever way I look the garden is a continuation, a green room beyond. There is neither in nor out: not for me or for the bees that take short cuts from window to window. Even the birds sometimes make no distinction, and a nightjar blinked throughout a summer morning from the top of a bookcase beside an image of the aged St Anne. The flowers in bowls, cool as those in the garden beds, stir like the curtains. Dry lavender and curled rose-petals smell as they once did out of doors. A vine, breaking against the house with the slap of a wave, throws its tendrils upwards, and gouts of green foam lie on the windowsills. Even the light is garden light. Reflected off the tiled floor, it makes patterns like lace, like rippling water, on the ceilings. The light is above you.

Looking out through the windows, I find more rooms: terraces and plots of green, walled with box hedges. To each terrace-room an inhabitant: on this, a taciturn apricot tree that speaks, giving fruit, once in five years; on that, a smooth-stemmed catalpa, like a reserved person in a green panama. Farther off, keeping their distance, are poplars, and they also stir like the curtains, the flowers in the bowls and the light on the ceiling. They rise haphazard; this from behind a wall of stone, that from behind a wall of lavender. The house is ringed with green spires. Their trembling confuses. Sometimes you hardly know from which window you are looking.

Beyond the green spires the first landscape waits. It seems a landscape in two parts: on one side, meadows and the river with its islands; on the other the abrupt hill, the *côte* as the natives called it, sinewy and dry. The house itself is a tidemark; the river-meadows lap to the garden wall and no farther. We are the frontier between the water-land and the chalk-land, and there is little natural movement across the border. If a stray bird, skimming the roofs, drops from the spare hillside into the green of the river-country, it drops into another world, like a stone into a pool.

The hillside with its combes stretches for many miles, overhanging river and meadows. I knew it first as an extension of the garden, entered through a gate beyond the orchard, where wasps crawled among the fallen fruit. The slopes were rough with scrub, and in the dips and sheltered places grew copses of wild cherry, red-berried ash, and birch. Anemones and orchids flourished on the chalk soil, and through thickets I stalked birds that to my imagination were more brightly coloured than flowers. Near the crest of the hill, where you could hear larks singing over the cornland above, the slope was broken by chalk bluffs and escarpments. Mysterious caves lay at their base, whose entrances were shadowed by trees and overhung by creepers. Owls and the black redstart nested there.

The hillside was wild. Adders basked in the sun and badgers outside their setts made mounds like miniature earthworks; in a sheltered combe I once startled a hind. It was on autumn mornings that the hillside felt most remote. A river mist, risen in the night like a tide, obscured the valley below and crept to the bases of the chalk bluffs. These were transformed into gleaming sea-cliffs, whence I looked over a tumbling white ocean. The fossil shells embedded in the chalk escarpments became sea shells, as it seems they once were, and the crows and hawks, sailing on the air-currents that eddied round the bluffs, became gulls and petrels, stooping as sea birds do into the troughs of the waves but rising with mist dripping from their wings. As the sun rose, the mist receded, leaving the hillside wringing wet. Rocks and shelving beaches emerged from an ebb tide. The trees glistened as though washed, and drops pattered from the leaves.

The hillside never lost this mysteriousness of autumn mornings. It was always other than might appear to a stranger scanning it from the valley below. Even its history was not immediately apparent. Though abandoned, it had been until a century earlier planted with vines and shored with dry walls whose lapsed remnants were here and there visible. It had known a regimented life. Husbandmen had dug, pruned and sprayed, moving month after month waist-deep among maturing grapes. Along zigzag paths children had carried up the midday meal, and down the same paths peasants at evening had returned. Nothing survived of this lost activity.

Apart from myself, only a blind man was familiar with every copse and cave and with the passage of days and seasons on the hillside. Old Battouflet had taken to the *côte* many years earlier and lent it his protection. With his mongrel bitch and his stick, he was there in all weathers and seemed part of it, an ambulating tree. Settling in a sheltered place, where a path took a turn below the ghost of a wall or to leeward of a clump of wild cherries, he would seem by the hour to scan the tide of air that washed over the valley. From such silent scrutiny he would break without warning into scabrous songs, his hoarse voice echoing along the slopes. Hearing his chants on summer afternoons when only the crickets competed, I made wide detours to avoid him – yet, when I thought myself undetected, he would hail me from the far side of a copse, as though effortlessly aware of my movements. He seemed to have uncanny knowledge of the *côte* and missed nothing that passed there. In time, as its only inhabitants, we became close friends in spite of the fifty years between us.

Though he was always out of doors, Battouflet's skin, seen usually through a grey stubble (he was shaved by a neighbour once a week), looked unhealthily white. Its pallor owed something to the high-domed, wide-brimmed straw hat that he wore summer and winter. It kept the light from his eyes. The latter had a detached look, contrasting with the sudden violence of his language and movements. In more than their blindness they were remote from the twitching grimaces that twisted his features. The eyes both fascinated and embarrassed me. Sometimes as I surreptitiously examined them they turned on me like burnt-out moons and I had the sensation of being intensely perceived.

The time came when I sought Battouflet daily on the *côte*. We greeted each other as partners, the sole proprietors of a large demesne, and I commonly began by giving him the latest news of our property. I spoke with conscientious detail; he listened and asked questions. The ravens, I said, were nesting as usual on the face of the big bluff and I judged the hen bird was sitting; a new badger sett was under construction below the hanging copse where I had seen a stoat the week before. The cave that we called the Owl Cave was unsafe; water and the ensuing frost had got into the massive lobe of chalk that overhung the entrance; it might come down at any time. When Battouflet talked it was little of his day's blind happenings. The hillside of which he spoke was something between the one I knew and the hillside he had once seen. He reverted to a vast oak which grew in his imagination. Rooted in a chalk escarpment, it leant into space, throwing shade on a copse far below. I searched for the tree; when I found its wreck, fallen years, perhaps decades, earlier, I dared not tell him. He also believed there were still bustard on the upland and that they sometimes strayed down the *côte*. He described them how they would run and then turn with an affronted stare and spread their tails. Each year he marvelled I had not seen them. 'You wait,' he said, 'autumn's the time; they're less wary then.'

He was versed in the lore of weather and of plants. Foretelling storm and calm, he could pronounce in February on the anemones, the *fleurs de Pâques*, and in April estimate the apricot harvest of June. Once in early summer I was bird's-nesting in the thickets below the bluffs when I heard the yapping of his mongrel Marguerite. Peering between the bushes, I saw him deep in conversation with one of the duke's keepers, a vacant boy. High in one hand he held a hare by the ears, while Marguerite kept jumping and barking. Cursing the dog, he struck at her vainly with his stick. The interruption barely broke the flow of his talk. Nodding his head for emphasis, he was giving instructions. The youth solemnly listened. Suddenly Battouflet turned in my direction and, as plainly as though he had seen me, shuffled the hare into his poacher's pocket. Marguerite sat back on her haunches puzzled at the sleight of hand. As I came into view, the boy eyed me uncertainly and turned to go. I heard Battouflet say, still nodding for emphasis, '*Broie le fin et assure-toi que le foie soit celui d'un daim.*' It was the prescription for some charm or love philtre. Once when I had been stung by wasps, he led me to a patch of herb and told me to rub the stings. It worked.

Battouflet's chief concern was the vegetation on the ghostly paths. Cutting and thrusting impatiently, his stick kept open a vestige of the vineyard tracks which would otherwise have been overgrown and lost. It was his single self-imposed task. His brown studies were often broken not only by raucous songs, but, more formidably, by his violent labours. Marguerite and I learnt to sit some feet away to avoid the stick which, without warning, would lacerate the air. Features and stick blindly working, he would ask, 'How is the path here, Robin, is it clear?' A stretch or two, once beaten hard by the husbandmen, he succeeded in keeping open, but often he would question me in some dell where barely the hint of a track remained. Torn and weeping suckers, trampled old man's beard and bruised bushes alone showed his handiwork. High summer, the time of his despair, was the time of his greatest activity. Day after day he would be out fighting the rank encroachment. The pressure of the flowing sap filled him with urgency. Slashing at the green, at the encircling tendrils and the advancing suckers, his stick worked like a scythe, mowing down the enemy.

Our hillside was limitless. Though I pushed far beyond Battouflet's territory, through trackless thickets and down tangled tracks where his flail had not fallen, it was never wholly explored. From copses of alder and birch that speckled me with shade and sun, I stumbled on unfamiliar places. From scrub where my head barely bobbed above a green surf, I emerged cocooned with gossamer and bindweed, decked with burrs and twigs. For assurance the valley was below. Lying on the smooth fringe of the bluffs, I saw the shrunken companionable fields that you could have ploughed with a toy, the motor-dot drawn as though without choice along the white road, the string of barges faintly chugging on the river, the hamlet that in perspective had only roofs, and our house itself, the talking poplars foreshortened and silent. Beside me, at eye level, insects laboured through grasses that seemed taller than the poplars and a purple anemone stretched ten miles across river and plain.

As I grew older summer became the season of the river. In the heat I deserted to the islands and the water. Seen from the *côte*, the river, placid and assured, curved in a generous horseshoe to the horizon; from the meadows you sensed rather than saw it. Tree-fringed and parcelled into channels between islands, you pieced it together from fragments, a whiteness under the willows, a vista between branches, a glint or a dark smoothness, now there, now gone. The volume of water in summer moved unobtrusively, and seemed not the same river as in the spring floods. Then it rose, almost as you watched, between denuded banks, submerging the islands, staining the fields a dirty brown. At full flood it swept through devastated root-crops and brought down poplars. On the islands, where the trees waded knee-deep, you heard woodpeckers laughing like water-birds. Sinking, the flood left jetsam and a film of mud. Branches, hung with battered tins, rags, long rubber fingers and scraps of paper, became hideous Christmas trees. Staves, bottles, and even chairs, were stranded in the fields. March was desolation. But as spring advanced the scars were hidden: at first barely veiled with decency under April gauze; later obscured by a new flood, the summer green. In June, the banks disappeared, and the river moved subdued between velvet curtains. The islands became jungles, and the voices of the cuckoos pulsed across the water on a medium denser than air. Sounds were muted. This was the real river, the timeless summer flow, on which my blue canoe floated out.

As my paddle bites into a smooth surface, circling eddies hurry downstream. The greenish water is deep and opaque. Shafts of sunlight falling between the trees explore only a foot beneath the surface, and show the water, like the air, full of wavering motes that drift out of sight. My hand trails in the river, submerges the round disc of a water-lily, and the water-boatmen skate away. The inside of the canoe is diapered with the shadow-pattern of leaves. In the sinuous channels that lead from one island to another, where the leaning trees meet above, it is still. There is only a private movement, cautious yet steady as a flow of traffic, a quiet coming and going: a snake crossing from island to island makes a wake like a toy boat; a butterfly wanders, yet purposefully, over the water; a moorhen paddles towards a patch of rushes, scrambles up the bank and disappears. As I ground on a sandspit, the canoe slews round and I am aware of the steady tug of the current. It keeps the scarves of river-weed in motion, and it draws gurgling and swelling off the prows of the islands. It seems as though the islands are thrusting upstream.

No one visits the islands, and after midsummer I force my way, as though storming a vessel, on to the tangles of floating green. Thigh-deep through the growth, where no one has been and no one will come again, I make my own path and leave a wake behind me. As I land, the nightingales and a single woodwarbler high above my head stop singing. I push into the silence. And then, for no reason, the birds begin again. I am cat's-cradled, threaded and cross-threaded with their songs; and I listen. I am threaded and cross-threaded by the sunlight falling through the leaves; and alone. Sometimes there are pauses, spaces, where the trees and vegetation hold back and the sunlight falls straight and deep as into a green well. Here I also pause, and at my feet am aware of a small traffic, smaller than the river traffic but as steady. I am aware of the beetle's dark forest and the centipede's precipice, and of pauses and spaces smaller than the still space in which I stand. Moving onward into the green, parting the green wall, I am lost again. The glint of water comes suddenly. I have crossed an island.

Beyond the last island lies the main stream, a languorous

expanse, where the swallows scud and soar. This is not a private river. On the far bank at Moisson the washerwomen thump their boards, and in midstream strings of barges move slowly to the monotonous 'chug, chug' that makes the rhythmical burden of summer days at Chantemesle. Brown fishing boats, moored between stakes, rock as the barges pass. The straw hats rock, and the rods, and the maggots in the tins, and the luncheon baskets. When things are going well, the fishermen shout to each other, '*Ça mord, hein!*' At other times they sit a long day in silence, only moving, with the same gesture and the same concentration, to cast afresh. Their rods make thin grey shadows on the water. If they look up, it is vaguely, as though dreaming. They do not see the sunlit stretches of the river or the polished launch with fluttering pennon. The girls in the rowing boat are half a mile away, and now they have drifted round the bend. The blue canoe has also disappeared.

It has turned with a long curved sweep of my paddle into channels behind the islands. It has left the barges and the fishermen, the deep current and the Moisson shore where the baker early on a Sunday morning waded out with his pockets full of stones. The blue has moved into the green and is lost. The blue is only visible to the moorhen peering from the banks. But down the quiet reaches it drifts a whole summer; and a whole summer the kingfisher pretends to doze on the dead branch. Below the sandspit, the scarf of weed swims, yet never moves. No other craft, it seems to me, floated in those waters.

❃ Two

THE HOUSE itself, the tidemark, was not mine like the hillside and the river. Long ago the green shutters had faded to aquamarine, and the hipped roofs, rippled as sea sand, barely contained the time that had accumulated there. Others had lived in the house before us. Their ghosts stirred the curtains, moved in and out of the rooms as easily as the bees. Where the valerian leant over the road and turned grey with summer dust, people sometimes stopped to read the tablet that my father put up: *Ce fût dans ce beau pays que le génie du peintre anglais Charles Conder s'est inspiré et dans ces lieux qu'il a trouvé son expression.* Though the gardener has long since died who said, '*Au temps de Monsieur Conder on ne buvait que du champagne,*' one of the cellars is still piled high with the bottles tossed there half a century ago. Across a wall in the dining-room, where Conder set them, proceed the mistresses of Louis XV, their poise unruffled. In the room beyond, his horseman, sweeping a tricorn hat, still rides through Seine orchards white with blossom, while the three gossamer shepherdesses, with panniered skirts and beribboned crooks, rise from their curtsy, light as birdsong: the three Miss Kinsellas from across the Atlantic, ghosts who once were courted here, and whose beauty, now fixed in Conder's pastoral, was the talk of the valley.

Wilde's shapeless figure, drinking *anis*, haunts one of the shady terraces. There on a hot August day he saw the man of letters bicycling down the road, saw the startled recognition, saw, as he wearily expected, the perspiring cyclist hesitate, wobble and turn back. As the figure pedalled away, they heard on the terrace something about principle in bicyclists being particularly commendable in August. But the edge of the wit is lost.

Whether Sarah Bernhardt first arrived in Conder's day, or later to visit his friend, the melancholy and handsome scholar, I never knew. In a box in the attic I found a crumpled velvet flower, which must have set off that imperious bosom, and a wad of letters. The confident handwriting was streaked and stained, and the mildewed pages hardly peeled one from another. As a child, I missed the passionate story but discovered among the letters a pamphlet, printed for friends, describing her first ascent in a balloon. I forget the year and the season, but for me it is always a spring day. I see the cheering crowd, a silk dress by Doucet, mauve gloves and mantle and a hat nodding with plumes like a prince's helm. As the mooring ropes are cast, she slowly rises in the bright light above the rapturous faces, as does the Virgin in her Assumptions. Drifting over Paris in the utter silence of balloon travel, they cut the *foie gras* and uncork the Pommery. Below, in the Bois, emerging from spring trees whose leafage seems to drift and curl like green smoke, frock-coated centaurs trot and prance on strips of yellow sand. On the Avenue, carriages move like ants, and the clip-clop of hooves is lost. Perhaps because I caught the note of admiration in older voices, I came to hear the swish of her silks on the steps that led from the studio to the garden, and imagined her holding there the regal pose which painters have recorded.

In a house where the air through open doorways drifted from

room to room, stirring the curtains, the branches of cherry and lilac and the flowers in the bowls, shades in high-buttoned jackets and singing dresses came and went without hindrance. Only when, surprised in their silent business, they dropped the *Revue Blanche* or concealed a copy of Arthur Symons's *Silhouettes* in the chest under the stairs, where the tennis racquets were kept, was their passage detected. They once left the 1899 wine list from Paillard's on the sideboard. The time had been, my father said, when their carriages drew up outside the green gates in the wall, the horses sweating, having left from the Abbaye de Thélème at dawn. Straight from the *cancan*, the black silk stockings and the taste of wine, the revellers woke with a start in full daylight, almost mid-morning, among cherry blossom. Years later people still enquired for them. Once or twice in the course of a summer the bell at the gates would clang and someone would ask uncertainly after this ghost or that. They left disconcerted, chilled by the consciousness of passing time, and aggrieved that friends, and perhaps more than friends, should die without a sign and the event leave no ripple. They foresaw their own deaths coming as a surprise to friend or lover making enquiry at a country house on a summer afternoon. The last of those for whom they enquired had indeed left, corporeally, in 1914 and with little time to pack.

My parents, who came after the war and found abandoned canvases and books, are now also ghosts, and they too move with the summer air in the rooms that they made their own. The loose-knit man, with grey-green eyes and hair that once was jet, drops his brush and in the studio stretches before his painting. He wears the room, as he wore most rooms, like a garment, a part of himself, and he surely greets the other shades – the air flows and ebbs like a tide, and there is the fall of footsteps and swish of dresses – with an abstracted kindness and solicitude. He so greeted the living. Pettiness never touched him. Yet as he views the world beyond the green spires, a puzzled look returns, as it often did, to his features. Perhaps it was this bewilderment that made him at last so much of a solitary, a man living at one remove.

I remember his tall figure leaning on the parapets of stone bridges, watching the dipping swallows and waiting for the evening rise. The same figure, but seeming even taller, stands at the tail of a long pool, a pillar in the sun patiently changing a fly, and with tried dexterity casts upstream to drop a Red Quill within two inches of the weed where a trout lies feeding. They knew him in Rochefort-en-Terre, Huelgoat and Questembert, and at Le Kloar he taught them to throw a fly. One summer evening the villagers gathered in the square and marvelled as time and again the line fell straight, the fly dropping coolly on the beaver hat that Jean-Pierre, his poacher friend, had placed far out on the cobbles. Though in my recollection he haunts the rivers of Brittany and the studio at Chantemesle, abstracted and something near sad, I wonder about a different man ringed with the colours of names that I heard as a child – the Atlas Mountains and the Sahara, Madeira, Capri, Munich – names which bore for me a magic connotation and which correspond, as I have learnt, to places on no map. It is a man I never knew, young and self-assured, wearing in some far-off spring the confident waistcoats and buttonholes that early photographs record, and with a charm women did not wish to resist. There was surely no sense of bewilderment, nor the later weariness, when he met my mother, who now shares with him the rambling house and terraces.

Like the shepherdesses she came across the Atlantic, but she holds her head more gracefully even than Conder's women, and her mind is quick and perceptive. For her, as for the three sisters,

Conder's cherry orchards remain in bloom, and whatever the season she carries white sprays and her baskets are full of flowers. They nod in her bowls and vases, and as she goes from room to room, where the lace-light trembles on the ceilings, there is a sense of expectation, of the beginning of June. On the terrace that is like another room, under the apricot tree, she gathers summer round her, and the progress of the months seems her achievement. Looking through the green spires to the world beyond, her glance meets all challenges. As she turns from the Sire de Gouberville, dead three hundred years, she copies on the edge of her manuscript, '*La vie n'est ni un plaisir ni une douleur, mais une affaire grave dont nous sommes chargés et qu'il faut conduire et terminer à notre honneur.*' Spirit informs the finely moulded features that at first sight seem as fragile as her flowers; it is this that holds the beauty, a beauty almost of youth, against the greying hair. One who so loved hillside and river, and the branches of blossom, is surely contented in these rooms. No rarer essence could haunt house or memory, or so enrich a first enduring scene.

❋ *Three*

I T WAS with the landscape that I grew and learnt. As the valley settles in time, it is veiled by a faint haze and the day is windless. Its life seemed tranquil to a child. The villagers were not suffering people. Their names were associated with a craft, a farm, or a particular strip of land, and not with worried lives. They had no passions but those echoed and deformed in words that adults spoke. Such a one 'loose', another 'avaricious'. Yet these people, figures and names less convincing to me than the fields they worked, were troubled; tempests of fear and passion raged in the windless afternoons. Spring, producing for me its sequence of amazement, exerted on cottage and farm a dour pressure. Recurring seasons, instead of pointing the wonder of the valley, must have obscured it. Dulling senses, crying, 'We have known this before,' knew always less. On the upland, in our hamlet under the bluffs, at Moisson across the river, distrust or apathy met the seasonal changes that I watched enthralled.

The hamlet like all places of habitation was under siege. Time was the enemy. For the garrison there were only sorties: a movement, camouflaged by green boughs, to secure the walnut crop; in September scattered spies foraging over the stubble with dogs and guns; the capture of new soil by the plough, rewarded with the ribbon of the *Mérite agricole*; the diversionary incident once a year on the square at Moisson, where booths and a pulsing merry-go-round recalled the triumph and martyrdom of the local saint, the only inhabitant to have escaped through the enemy lines; or, bravest and most desperate show, the long white table set with wine and food under the trees by the river to celebrate a marriage. But the hamlet was invested and the siege continued. My valley was the terrain across which treacherous seasons advanced. Their passage killed or, more cruelly, hid life behind ever-thickening barriers of experience.

The young understand pain but are as untouched by tragedy as the innocent by vice. I watched mere event: at Moisson, the cripple with dangling legs jerking down the street on crutches; Madame Bertrand weeping, whose jaunty son was knifed in a Paris flat ('*Il avait des mauvaises fréquentations,*' the sinister phrase remains); Jean slumped behind his bar, struck with an apoplexy; and the end of Mademoiselle Firmin.

The Firmins were our closest neighbours. The dispirited father, a widower who wore carpet slippers in the garden, had in some prosperous and distant time built a villa on one of the islands. He had intended a pleasance, but in his needy retirement was constrained to live there the year round. His daughter kept house for him. Mademoiselle Firmin, a shrunken woman of fifty with a stringy neck and a moustache that showed against the extreme whiteness of her skin, was intelligent. It was an unripened, sad intelligence. Her thoughts and gestures were tentative. She swallowed before she spoke, and she dressed in the unsuitable black clothes which in those days ladies of the French upper-middle class dared not discard even on an island. Les Nénuphars was a pleasant house in summer, and as my canoe drifted past I heard the sound of the mower on the lawns 'spurting its little fountain of vivid green'. A garden on an island meant that close to the banks you paddled below flower-beds. Ripe fruits plopped into the water. As they bobbed down the current, you could put out a hand and grab sopping pears and plums. The ornamental trees, fringing the banks like an openwork screen, seemed to drift and move only less swiftly than the canoe. As their trunks alternately hid and revealed parts of the garden, the same clump of flowers would reappear, and each time seem different.

Winter was another matter. The river hurried by, the lush vegetation was gone and the island grew dank. When the trees lost their leaves, the villa could be seen marooned in an empty garden, its windows looking sadly across the current towards the mainland. Sometimes house and garden vanished, wrapped in river mists. When the vapour lifted, it left them bathed in a cold perspiration. From bare branches there was a steady drip, drip, into the water. For weeks at this season the only news from the island was the clanging bell that summoned their boatman to the landing-stage when Mademoiselle Firmin went shopping at Vétheuil. As he ferried her across the river, her skimpy black figure sat retracted in the stern. It seemed that wisps of mist still clung to her as she stepped with shopping-bag into the Léon-Bollet. Winters were difficult at Les Nénuphars.

The father died one February and my parents in the following months asked Mademoiselle Firmin to Chantemesle more frequently than they would otherwise have done. They derived little pleasure from her visits. Sitting uneasily in the drawing-room, she presented a blanched and uncommunicative face. There was no appeal for sympathy. At tea she ate a single sandwich, and this with an appearance of effort. After an hour's talk of local affairs, she took her handbag, gave a brief shake to her black dress, and left. The boatman rowed her, hands folded in her lap, across to the empty villa.

Swimming at Chantemesle belonged to the ritual of summer. The Seine below Paris is a dubious green, but to me it seemed cool and welcoming. At first with a grown-up in attendance and later alone, I rowed out to bathe in a blunt-nosed fishing-boat. When my cousins came to stay there were four of us. Leaning over the sides, clambering on the prow, never still, we must have looked, as we drew from the shore, like creatures caged behind invisible bars, fretting for the cool element beneath us. There must have been a repeated echoing across the water as we shouted and laughed. When we broke free, diving it seemed simultaneously and at a preconcerted signal, there was a brief surprising silence. Our restlessness transferred to the water, it became aswirl, eddying, spouting and throwing ripples against the bank and the side of the boat. Our favourite bathing-place was off the end of the Firmins' island, and sometimes in the summer of which I speak Mademoiselle Firmin under her parasol watched us intently from the lawn. 'Come and join us, Mademoiselle Firmin,' we shouted, thinking it a great joke. She only waved. A moment later she would disappear among the trees, leaving us in possession of the river.

One day late in the season she announced, as though it were wholly natural, 'Perhaps I shall accept your invitation. It would be nice to bathe again. I used once to swim a good deal at Trouville.' We did not take her seriously until a note arrived for my mother. When, Mademoiselle Firmin asked, was the next bathing party and might she join the children? My mother with surprise replied that we should be bathing next day after tea. To tea Mademoiselle Firmin came, carrying an embroidered bag that contained her bathing-suit and wrap. She put it beside the chair where the table was set in the shade of the apricot tree. When my father called her a *sportive*, she turned with so pained an expression and an involuntary gesture of such distaste that it took us aback. 'Now, children, don't eat too much,' said my mother to change the subject. 'It's not good for you before bathing.' It was too hot to eat much; a sweltering day gave little breeze even on the terrace. We had soon finished. But Mademoiselle Firmin did not finish. When the last sandwich had disappeared and the macaroons, she turned to one of Ada's great layered cakes whose richness compelled even our respect. We watched her in amazement. Usually so frugal, she attacked it with determination, carrying morsel after morsel with short rapid motions to a pursed mouth that opened and closed obediently. One huge slice disappeared, a second and then a third, and when each was finished she drew a cambric handkerchief from her bag and wiped a rime of chocolate from her lips. She gave the impression of someone performing an unpleasant task, and we children who had been on the verge of giggles were silenced. While we stared, my mother tried to keep up conversation. Mademoiselle Firmin answered at random, her chops moving steadily, her eyes fixed on the hillside above. It was with an effort that she brought them back to the table, viewed the diminished cake, and cut a fourth slice. Even for her strong purpose this proved too much. She took a bite and then with a look of nausea pushed her plate away. A moment later, with the air of someone whose work is finished, she gave the customary shake to her black dress. 'Such a delicious tea,' she said, 'but I am afraid my appetite has quite run away with me . . . I am ready whenever the children are.'

She was a long time undressing in the boathouse. My father had predicted a period costume, something striped with frills and pantaloons, such as was usual before the First World War. When she appeared it was in a new bathing-dress. Far too large, and no doubt chosen for this very reason, its black serge hung in folds; yet probably never before had she exposed so much of her body. There were blue veins below her thighs, and her legs were straight, almost without calf. We were obscurely sorry for her, but scrutinised her with interest. Stepping into the boat she stumbled and it rocked, sending ripples over the dry round discs of the lilies. Though the trees were already throwing shadows across the water, it was a bright, tranquil evening. The thwarts where we sat in our bathing-slips retained a warmth from the day's sun. She shivered. '*Eh bien! nous voilà, mes enfants,*' she said with a pained smile. 'She's got the wind up,' someone whispered; 'You see, she won't bathe after all.' We drifted out on the current, pulling the oars from time to time to keep straight. As so often before, we anchored below the Firmin island. The water downstream shone smooth and polished, giving no hint of its depth or of the silt, and worse, that it was carrying seaward. It tantalised with the promise of exertion and pleasure. 'Come on, Mademoiselle Firmin,' we said, and showing off we shattered the gleaming surface in quick succession. A moment later we were looking back at the boat expectantly. As though cold or modest, she sat with arms crossed over her chest and her hands on her shoulders. At last she got up and lowered herself slowly down the steps that hung from the stern. Then, giving a self-conscious wave, she launched out and began to swim deliberately downstream. She had a stilted, old-fashioned action and held her chin high as if she could not bear the water to touch her hair. The head bobbed away from us at each stroke, moving into the swifter current. Looking out of place, with the greying hair piled on top and the white neck that seemed never to have known the sun, it drew sedately away; and then, as we watched, it disappeared. We waited for it to re-emerge. Heads we knew always re-emerged, the face spluttering and smiling. We waited in vain.

The end of Mademoiselle Firmin was an incomprehensible episode that left me startled. I wondered to hear someone say her death was 'the best thing that could have happened', but I missed the sense of tragedy and of the grey years that had preceded it. It was not long before we were bathing again and in the following summer we returned to our favourite stretch below the Firmin island. It was the best place we knew.

Reality was not in such tragedies, but in the passage of hours, days and seasons across the Chantemesle landscape. I lived in a valley of my own and in a time that seemed timeless. On spring mornings before dawn I stood in the garden tranced by the birds' chorus. I seemed to be listening to myself and to the whole valley. A quarter-mile away, until the leaves came to muffle sound, the woodwind of a dozen thrushes was audible on the islands. From the hillside the melancholy note of a tree pipit, as it circled downward to its station on a thorn tree, lured me up the terraces, across the still orchard and through the gate. Beyond, another note would draw me. So I strayed, always farther, until the volume of song diminished and the day was there.

'Tranced' is the appropriate word. I often stood looking or listening in amazement. On a windless day by the river I would find that bellying white clouds had inexplicably appeared above the hilltop and halt in my tracks. Again and again I was halted on the hillsides themselves by the wetness of the dew and the morning freshness, by the heat ticking like a clock at noon, or by the star that surprised me (with daylight still there) above the combes and bluffs. Even now the wild cherries on the slopes, beautiful and useless, that duly flowered in those Aprils will break a train of thought. Once almost anything would work the spell: a fern, a snail shell, the gloss of new chestnuts or a glowworm in the palm of my hand as I went up to bed. I remember crinkling the sloughed skin of a snake, and staring transported at the secret scribbles on a bunting's egg. One autumn afternoon under a leaden sky, the gardener was burning the yellow grass in the orchard. I watched the flames creep up the hill under the twisted apricot trees. They left the ground shorn, like a black lamb fleeced. As I walked over the woolly substance, the ash dissolved in powder under my feet. Looking back, I saw my footprints on the hillside.

❧ *Four*

A THIRD ELEMENT of the landscape, which I came to know after the hillside and the river, was the upland that rolled away from the top of the bluffs. It was all air. Larks rose above a corn sea and yellowhammers called monotonously beside rutted tracks. Stabbing the sky, the spires of village churches were the only signposts from one horizon to another. As you walked, even these points of reference shifted. There was nothing to maintain a sense of direction, one cornfield followed another and the flowers were always poppy and scabious. Everywhere the same larks rose, the same yellowhammers spoke and the same covey of partridges settled on the edge of a field. Even the occasional spinneys resembled one another. With sun ironing out the colour and wind scudding over the thirsty wheat, it was a pale landscape, without the rich contrasts of the valley. Yet it impressed by very emptiness. The wheat seas lured and the spires beckoned. Though Battouflet's bustards eluded me, I was content there to see all day nothing different, nothing new.

In such country, the lake was the only surprise. Its explanation lay in the green hummocks that spoke of a medieval house or abbey, for it had been dammed in a distant past. There were rainbow trout, and my father went often to fish; for me the attraction lay in the place itself. Uplifted and open, the lake induced a sense of buoyancy. It seemed natural that the sky, of which there was so much, should be reflected in the water. White clouds drifted on the surface as confidently as above our heads. Except for hawthorns and stocky willows that lined the banks and proved a constant fishing hazard, there were no trees. Whizzing swallows flicked the surface and I sometimes mistook the widening circles for rising trout. Sandpipers minced on gravel spits, and at the head of the lake a pair of great crested grebes cruised near the reed-bed where they nested. Watching them dive, I tried to guess where they would reappear from the oozy bottom. With a shake of feathers, they always broke water where least expected.

Below the lake the cornland stretched without feature but for the shifting spires. It was easy to stray into unfamiliar country. One afternoon, following a track from field to field, I came to the lip of a miniature valley. It wound steep-sided through the upland. Strips of lush meadow made a level bottom and lay so near the water-table that in places they were bounded with rushy dykes. Elsewhere solid post-and-rail fenced them. Bloodstock grazed there, unlike the serv- iceable horses I knew. Splendid creatures, dominating their pastures, they made me uneasy. Beyond this pause of meadow, a narrow belt of trees rose; they were outlined against the farther hillside. In their shade, where the stallions must have stood, was bare earth and the buzzing of horseflies. Branches swept the ground so that animals there would have been invisible from the pasture.

A stream ran under the trees and I heard the swish of the current before I saw it. The water moved fast; scarves of weed wavered upward and were jerked down. Here were no reflections of white clouds, but hints of green and purple. Where an alder had fallen, a surface scum backed uneasily against the boughs and an eddy sucked at the flotsam. The watercourse was edged with boards to prevent flooding, and in places the current, seeping between the boards, had formed miniature lagoons outside. These were clear and still by contrast with the current. I could see drowned twigs, leaves and kingcups on the grassy bottoms. Perhaps it had rained higher up the valley or a sluice-gate had been opened. Following the stream, I made it a point of honour not to retreat from its verge, balancing my way on the upright boards between the current and the lagoons. I could sometimes do so only by steadying myself with a hand on the boughs above.

I had gone some half-mile when I realised that the belt of trees was coming to an end. Beyond, in a circle of light, as if seen through the end of a telescope, a boy sat fishing where a water-meadow bordered the stream. In the background rose a seemly house, solid and self-assured, with newly painted green shutters. I had an impression of ornamental trees, of raked gravel, of statues on plinths beside a lawn and of geraniums trailing from high stone urns. I turned aside, but as I reached the meadows the boy confronted me. His skin was pale, his ears lobeless, and his coarse hair grew low on the back of his neck; but he was handsome, with full lips and large features.

'Who are you?' he said.

'I came down the stream.'

'This is private,' he said. 'It's ours . . . You must leave.'

Something made me stiffen. 'I shall go on down the stream if I want to.'

'Then the keeper will throw you in . . . or I shall stab you.' He drew a sheath-knife from his belt. He had enormous hands for a boy and his waistless body was solid. 'I often stab people.'

I backed away; not much, yet years later I remembered with

regret that it was a little. As I did so a woman called shrilly from the steps of the house, 'Clovis . . . Clovis.' He paused, and we were both glad of the intervention.

'Foreign', he said contemptuously and walked away.

I pondered this odd meeting as I made for home. Though the setting sun had dropped behind a bank of cloud before I reached our hillside, I went at once to consult Battouflet in his single-roomed cottage.

Some rooms are like lizards' crannies: their owners scuttle for refuge behind angular furniture. Others, with stinking pipes in racks, are the setts of old badgers. Others are dormice rooms, hibernatories with heavy curtains, where the gas-fire purrs for months and the book slides from the inert hand. Some are squirrel rooms full of food-money, larders of Fabergé eggs, nuts of lapis lazuli, *pâté* of porphyry and *giallo antico* butter, all put aside against a rainy day. Some are peacocks' rooms full of mirrors, where there is no escaping the human figure and even mahogany reflects a face. There are also false rooms, decoys like the false nests that wrens build. Battouflet's cottage was like the form of a hare: he no more lived in it than a hare lives in a depression in a clover field. It was a sleeping and resting place when necessity drove him from the hillside or from Chez Jean, the inn on the outskirts of the hamlet. Three strides took you across his room into an unkempt patch of garden. Nothing grew there but weeds, a few potatoes and an unpruned rose tree. A wooden butt that collected rainwater from the roof lent a damp smell to the enclosure. Newts swam in it.

The cottage lay slightly below road level, so that you stepped down over the stone threshold. Passers-by would see him sitting in his form, sideways to a deal table, and avert their eyes from his stare. He would interpret and greet the step of friends, for like a hare he heard everything, and when enemies passed, which was more usual, he would tap impatiently with his stick on the earthen floor and Marguerite would growl. His perceptions seemed especially clear at dusk, and on the evening that I came to find him he called my name when I was still some way off. I took the only other chair in the room and pulled it to the opposite side of the table. His stick became active when I brought unusual news. 'What's happened?' he said. 'You ought to be at home now.' Of course he knew the little valley and the house, but the name puzzled him. 'Clovis, Clovis,' he said. 'The only person who ever bore that name was old Monsieur de Chérence in the forest over the river. He died years ago.'

Battouflet as a boy, and his father before him, had been employed on Monsieur de Chérence's estate. It was his earliest landscape, and through it rode Armand, the one-eared huntsman, who still lived in his thoughts. The missing ear had been torn off in an epic passage through the forest, and there was no story of the huntsman's cunning which I did not know, or of Rosinante, the shapeless roan of seventeen hands whose appearance belied a wild courage. Battouflet often spoke of the forest, of its giant ants, of its curious white strawberries large as medlars, of the savage boars, of the heronry with its sentinel birds on guard day and night, and of the house with its towers and battlements set, like the heronry, in the depth of the woods. During the hunting season even the servants had feasted three nights a week on boar and venison. Though the people of whom he spoke, with the exception of the aged Madame de Chérence, were now dead, the persons of this vanished community were as clear to him as if they lived.

A month or two after my meeting with the boy, Clovis, I was sitting with Battouflet on the hillside. It was a still autumn day with a tang in the air, one of those majestic days when the ageing globe seems to draw away from the sun in resignation. The slopes below us, the house ringed with poplars, the river and the wide landscape beyond, were unusually clear. Sound travelled easily, and we heard the altercation of crows half a mile away, black dots on a freshly ploughed field.

The curtains that once draped a summer river had changed their colour and texture. Hangings of stiff gold damask, veined with black and flaring into red or burnt sienna, were now reflected on the water, where sprinklings of curled leaves moved downstream like fleets under sail. On the far bank, at Moisson, tiny figures crossed the street from one house to another, and doorways swallowed them. Their coming and going was arbitrary unless one knew the significance of each house. With such knowledge, I could safely say to Battouflet, 'The butcher has crossed the street into the café. The doctor has gone over to Madame Dubois.' Beyond the small activity of the village, the plain stretched to the Chérence forest. Isolated by a wide loop of the river, and traversed by a single empty road, the plain was at all times deserted. In the autumn sunlight it looked more so than usual. Like the forest beyond, it seemed to exist out of time.

Battouflet, as I have said, often gave the impression of staring fixedly at the views which he could not see, and which from our vantage on the hillside were spread generously before him. As we sat in silence, he stiffened. From far out, from somewhere in the forest, we heard on the still air, faintly repeated, the note of a horn. Not the peremptory note of the English hunting horn, but that of the sweeping instrument handled by the huntsmen who canter across the tapestries of Louis XV. Battouflet strained to catch the sound and his features worked as they always did when he was disturbed. With my clear sight, I quartered the plain and the forest. Nothing moved;

but then an army could have lain in the forest undetected. Battouflet shook his head. Madame de Chérence was a cripple, her kennels had been empty and the deer untroubled for twenty years. 'It might be Monsieur Didot's hounds from the Epte valley; it's a long way, but perhaps ... ' We waited listening, but in vain. No further signal reached us.

Though the autumn day moved gravely on and the view was precisely the same, I felt that something momentous had occurred. With the sounding of this horn, the forest had come to life. As the notes died away, 'beyond the river' became a reality. The widespread view, so long the still background to the prospect from the hill, stirred in my imagination and I sensed all that moved invisibly under the trees. As though he realised, Battouflet said, 'One day you must go to Chérence.'

The hunting horn, if it were such, reverberated in Battouflet's mind through the winter. He spoke repeatedly of the forest and its inhabitants. None of his stories were forgotten. I noted the words people had uttered, the deeds they were reputed to have done. When in the woods, long after, I met a dwarflike ranger, I knew him at once for the son of a hunchback whom Battouflet had fought. I even found a new significance in the stray herons that I met on the river. They became messengers of portent, like the birds and animals, sometimes gifted with speech, which in fairy stories guide the youngest son to his goal.

From the hillside I watched the leaves fall, and the forest, stamped on the plain like a great irregular birthmark, change from brown to purple-grey. With the coming of winter, the evergreens – cedars and holm-oaks as I afterwards discovered – asserted their presence. Later, in the course of a single March day, a pinkish powder dusted the woods. Soon after came the first washes of green, diaphanous, drifting like mist. Then I looked again: mist and trees had gone. An opaque green tide had rolled across the plain and engulfed the forest. So at a distance I learnt something of its nature, as travellers before setting out read in books of the changing appearance of the tundras or of the effects of climate in Luristan.

❧ *Five*

I WENT in deep summer. Not even Battouflet knew of my going, and I announced an expedition to the islands in search of butterflies. Though I left the house in the freshness of early morning, the day promised heat. Fruit and *pain au chocolat* were in my pocket. From the encircling poplars, I went down to the river and pushed out the canoe. At Moisson, I passed through the village and beyond the last orchards entered the plain. The soil, poor and sandy, was not worth cultivating. Only in the First World War had a use been found for the plain as a dirigible base. Abandoned in the ling or wrapped in brambles were rusting shapes not easily explained, and I crossed a large naked patch, bare as if a searing iron had been pressed against the earth and the dead skin had refused to grow again. The positive feature in the landscape, that which led me steadily on, was the forest verge rising like a wall. As I approached, its solid formality disappeared; the wall gave place to a coastline, varied and individual, with bays and promontories. In its cliffs were grottoes and caverns into which the sun flowed like a tide. I drew closer and the cliffs dissolved into trees, into trunks and canopies of leaves. The brown birthmark on the autumn plain, the grey lichen-like expanse of winter, the tide of green, the wall, the forest, all these became simply a multitude of branches and leaves. A jay screamed at me, and a flicker of colour passed into the depths. I was close now. The shadow of a giant oak spread almost to my feet. I turned to look back across the plain and river at the familiar hillside. There it was in faithful miniature: the warped roofs of our house just visible, the green spires, the orchard, the curt steep *côte* and the bluffs above. Yet how unfamiliar it appeared; neither more nor less imposing; but different. So on the forest edge came to me obscurely a new sense of perspective, of distance making the familiar strange, and of landscapes changing.

I walked towards the oak tree. I was knee-deep in its shadow, waist-deep, my head alone was in the sunlight; then I passed into the wood. At first I moved like a trespasser, stepping carefully. But the green welcomed me. In the breathless air the trees rode the undulating sward like becalmed vessels, and I passed safely beneath their towering hulks. Where ships had foundered in tremendous storms, wrecks encumbered the ground, impeding my passage. In most places, however, there was, at first, little undergrowth. Sometimes I emerged into natural clearings which, as though set for a masque, seemed to be awaiting my entrance. When I halted on the threshold of such green-papered rooms I realised how illusory was the silence. As I ceased to move, the forest, as if a current at that exact moment were turned on, began to shimmer and vibrate. What had appeared still was full of activity. The air hummed with insects, a hornet whizzed past, deadly as a bullet, a woodpecker beat a tattoo and hesitated as though expecting reply, pigeons broke clattering from their bowers, squirrels swung from tree to tree and a hare loped away. Pausing once in this fashion, I heard a rustling and saw the very ground was in motion. One of Battouflet's giant anthills, several feet high, lay not far off. Absorbed in their tasks, the lumbering ants, different from the nervous little creatures usually met with, clambered about their Great Pyramid or hauled their gross white eggs into deep chambers. As I twisted and turned a stick in the rustling mound, the sudden acceleration and frantic motion of thousands of ants changed the tone of the faint note that rose from the anthill. It was as though a high-pitched scream reached my ears.

When I stopped to eat, the day had grown hot. I was far from home and might have turned back, but the heart of the forest – which I envisaged as a spot perfectly defined and unmistakable when found – drew me on. The trees now closed their ranks. The wrecks which I had noticed earlier and the dilapidation of the forest – for it was badly in want of a forester's care – produced the effect of jungle. Progress was difficult. When at last trees and undergrowth parted it was to show me a stretch of tousled rushes, dotted with clumps of mauve flowers. These had attracted swallowtail butterflies that fluttered aimlessly back and forth or settled on the blooms, expanding and closing their black and yellow wings. Swampy ground under my feet squelched and oozed. Pushing onward, I barked my shin. Beneath green wrappings I found, as in a cocoon, a rustic garden-seat that seemed waiting for someone to sit on it. An ornamental lake must have existed where the reeds now grew, and here people had watched wildfowl sailing on a placid water. As I pondered the exciting conjunction of seat and jungle, I realised that I was observed from the heart of the reed-bed. A yellow eye followed my progress around the swamp with curiosity. A moment later, on slow wing beat, a bird, white as snow, rose from the reeds with dangling legs, lifted over the trees and was gone. I did not grasp that I had seen the Great White Heron. But I knew that here was a species figured in none of my books and I had a feeling that the meeting was prearranged, that the bird had been awaiting me, in the depths of this forest on a summer afternoon.

Beyond the swamp, where the trees closed in again, I came abruptly on a forest ride. Its walls were trimmed, showing the first signs that I had seen of human care. Preparing to slip into the wood beyond, I looked upwards. This time it was a ruby eye that fixed me, provocative and brilliant. A head that should have been in Niger jungles turned on one side and summed me up; then with a perfunctory scream the parakeet sailed out of sight. Birds played a large part in my life and these apparitions seemed miraculous.

Beyond the ride, oaks and sycamores towered over a wilderness of hazels that grew close as a curtain. Wading through the fluffy foliage, I bumped against an iron grille. The bars nearly as thick as my wrist rose straight for some ten or twelve feet and then curved out of sight. They seemed to mark no boundary, for the hazels flowed past them without pause, as a stream flows past the uprights of a bridge. Growing impartially on either side, the hazels ignored the barrier. I was unable to do so. Looking for a passage, I realised that the grille was part of a large iron cage. With difficulty I made my way to a corner. The interior angle was still spanned by a substantial perch from which hung a rusting chain. Bald vultures or dusty buzzards had once dozed there. So thick were the hazels that I turned the corner before realising that there were now bars on either side of me. I was in a passage between two of these disused aviaries. Others lay beyond. Long abandoned they had been taken over by the forest. The original occupants had gone, but now humbler birds – magpies, jays and warblers – had succeeded to the quarters, flitting in and out between the bars whence the wire-netting had perished. The captive was myself, picking a bewildered way through a labyrinth of leaves and iron.

When I stumbled on a path, the cages seemed hallucination. The green had swallowed them. The path, one of those walks that proclaim the nineteenth century, was well kept, its cambered surface weeded and its edges clipped. Self-conscious in its windings, it led me successively past a stone urn and a bronze boar, the very same had I but known as Pietro Tacca copied for Ferdinando de' Medici. The forest was changing; there was a sense of approach and of preparation. Yet I was taken by surprise when the path, upon a flourish, suddenly confronted me with formal parterres, lawn and house.

Turrets and crocketed pinnacles, rising like stalagmites with a bold disregard for symmetry, broke the roofline. From a dozen summits as many weather vanes, conceived as escutcheons, bore the arms of the owner. They were motionless that summer afternoon. At different levels, brief stretches of castellation were indiscriminately applied, recurring motifs upon the structure, like fragments of lace trimming on a dress. The impression of fretted fantasy was emphasised by window-balconies, painted white, like those provided in stage-sets for the exchanges of a romantic duet. Elsewhere oriel windows suggested bowers to which the singing lovers might retire. The fenestration was purely picturesque: some windows, I later discovered, served no room at all, while other rooms were in perpetual twilight.

No surface, whether of stone or tile or bold half-timbering, was without decoration: here a sundial so high upon the wall that no one might read it; there a Gothic canopy sheltering the recumbent figure of a knight; elsewhere, bright as the flowers in the parterres below, a tessellated riband displaying the flowing legend, *Sois pur sous les cieux, comme l'onde et l'aurore.* Flanking the front door were two enormous flambeaux, fitted with gas burners. Wayward and irrational, half-castle yet related to the sugar-icing cottage of fairy tales, the house was all that I could desire, for I was still of an age impervious to the tyranny of taste. The latter would have approved only the balustraded terrace, the relic of an earlier building, and the vista where an avenue, set in parkland hemmed on either side by forest, stretched into the distance.

Though the house seemed deserted, I hesitated. I had reached 'the heart of the forest' and it was late. I could return another day. It was then I heard a man's voice, close yet disembodied, floating out of green leaves:

> '*Les costeaux soleillez de pampre sont couvers,*
> *Mais des Hyperborez les éternels hyvers*
> *Ne portent que le froid, la neige, et la brume.*'

As though it had waited to deliver its commentary, a blackcap broke the silence that followed.

The voice resumed:

'The *Pléiade* is an appropriate name for these poets, not so much because they were in number like the stars in the constellation – Electra, the dim star that is always in mourning, Maia, Merope and the rest – but because their words are clear and still shine . . . You can write that down . . . "Their words are clear and shine like starlight." '

Through the branches, where a strip of lawn, smooth as a creek, ran back into the wood, I could see a thatched summer-house, already half in shadow. A girl, bent over an exercise book, was sitting at a wrought-iron table and an old man in a basket chair gazed into the trees. His face was more skeletal and elongated than those of the saints I had seen in the porches at Chartres. A mere film of skin covered the bones of cheeks and forehead and the long ridgepole of his nose. His ears were as though carved in horn or discoloured ivory, while his narrow hands (and one was now raised as if he were touching the sunlight) looked almost transparent. Even his greying beard was thin, as though there were not flesh enough on his jowl to nourish a stronger growth. His clothes hung so loosely on his frame that but for his eyes, which flashed from their caves, it might have been a puppet there, cloth, sticks and wire. 'Clotilde,' he said. The girl looked up; the hair that framed her face was jet and as she sat with her head on one side in an attitude of question it fell on her page, burying the hand which held the pencil. The face with its olive skin was arresting, and seemed to share something indefinable with the fleshless features upon which the girl concentrated her attention. Both faces gave the impression – it is hard to describe more precisely – of not being contemporary. It was as if these two were free denizens of a world, a private dimension, where the common inevitabilities were of no account and where the laws that imprison us all were in suspense.

As I leaned forward, screened by the leaves, a branch snapped under my foot. The girl turned sharply. Though invisible I had the same sensation of scrutiny as on the edge of the swamp under the gaze of the white heron. She threw down her pencil and called angrily in my direction, 'Clovis'. The old man shut the book on his knees. It was as if the presence of a third person had broken a closed circuit. 'Clovis!' she called again, and a chock of wood that propped open the summerhouse door crashed through the leaves and fell at my feet. I turned and ran, hearing, as I went, branches breaking behind me.

When at last I paused, conscious of the beating of my heart, the footsteps had ceased, but as I listened a distant cry echoed through the wood, '*Sale bête*.' A briar had scratched the back of my hand and blood welling to the surface traced a red line, fluent as the stroke of a pen. What, I wondered, brought Clovis to these woods?

When I took my bearings, the nature of the forest had once more changed. Through open glades where the sun cast long shadows and through shafts of light, in which the wings of insects glinted, I steered for home. A small breeze, the first that day, with the gentle yet firm persistence of an incoming tide, explored the depths of the forest. I felt it on my face before noticing the faint movement of the leaves. After the heat and hush of the last hours, the woods relaxed. About me there was an easy coming and going on padded feet and on wings. Birds, aimless and graceful, swooped in the cool across my path. Their disappearance as they passed from sunlight into shadow was instantaneous. When I halted, there at my feet, as if specially for me to find, lolling back on their ribbed leaves were two or three of the forest's pallid strawberries. They must have been the last of the season.

❋ *Six*

IN DIFFERENT CIRCUMSTANCES I often returned to Chérence. I
became free of the hazel thickets and the abandoned aviaries, of
the reed-bed and the glades where the trees sailed like ships. I learnt
the names of the exotic birds that screeched in the rides, and knew
my way in the remote parts of the forest. Yet the latter did not grow
commonplace. Things at Chérence continued to bear an unusual
signature. Catching sight of my arm and hand resting on a bough I
discovered, with a sense of revelation, that I was other than myself.
'But this hand is not my hand,' I said and looked about me as though
awaking. 'This hand is not my hand': the inadequate phrase recalls
the wonder, the sense of things being other than they seemed, that
attached to everything in the forest.

Though I did not repeat the laborious route across the plain, the
traverse of the river was inescapable. Separating the forest from my
familiar world, it was a decisive step to somewhere different. I usually
crossed at La Roche, a village three or four kilometres from home.
Luca, our squat and devoted Italian whom my mother had brought
from the Abruzzi, would drive me to the strand where the boats were
moored.

The river at La Roche was unlike my river upstream. Fast but silent, the Seine moved in a broad flood. There were no islands or creeks. Nor was there a blue canoe; only cumbersome fishing boats, with blunt prows. To counteract the current and reach the landing stage on the opposite bank, I had to start by rowing upstream. A moment arrived when I was isolated, lost on the slipping expanse, alone with the creak of the rowlocks and the splash of the heavy blades. There was a confusing glare off the water; extent and brightness dizzied me. Closing my eyes, or looking steadfastly into the bottom of the boat, I pulled hard at the oars. Suddenly – it was always sudden – the current ran slower and a few yards away trees leant over the Chérence bank. Feeling that a frontier had been crossed, I stepped on shore exhilarated, but still dazzled by the river light. So I always started for the house a little giddy, shaking my head to get rid of the brightness.

It was natural that I should have got to know Clotilde soon after my first visit to Chérence. The few children in our part of the valley met each summer, combed, frilled and starched, at various houses for fêtes and *goûters*. The seasonal ritual, set in motion by our parents, drew us like a flock of twittering birds, and armed like birds in beak and claw, to terraces and lawns, dispersed us under heavy August trees, or set us to dance, self-conscious and suddenly older, round gilt drawing-rooms where formal Louis XVI chairs were ranged against the walls. In this ritual Clotilde and I met. So began the friendship which dominated the three years that followed. Though she played so large a part in my life it is difficult for me to describe Clotilde, the admired being who sponsored me in her landscape, and drew me with a sense of privilege into the life of the forest. I can see the solemn look, the smile that in a child was almost melancholy, and recall the unusual grace of movement that enabled her to pass like a shadow down the rides or slip unobserved through a plantation. A single image visits me faithfully, capricious only in the times of its appearance: I see Clotilde's dark hair hanging down her back, and I see it from behind as she moves through the close green of the woods; then the hair disappears, and there is only the agitation of leaves, the momentary nodding of boughs, indicating the way I must follow. There was no first love between us, and in the long run time spared little of our friendship. She was never to be moved by men. In life, as through our unfolding forest, Clotilde followed her own paths.

Miss Partridge, efficient and opinionated, controlled the surface of life at Chérence. Her word was a law we privately questioned but always pretended to obey. Living long abroad had gallicised the governess's manners and tastes and had led her to forget much of her own country. Only her prejudices remained distinctively English, and these resulted in her continually saying and doing things which seemed out of her acquired character. Luckily she approved of me. Approval rested on the belief that English boys were fitter companions for girls than foreigners. Her animosity had banished Clovis, the cousin whose name I knew so well, and it was uneasily that I learnt of his simple misdemeanours. The information was given as a warning.

Miss Partridge's authority was subject only to the grandmother, Madame de Chérence. Though of great age the latter still seemed a big woman, and too large for her wheelchair. Her sight was failing and, as a consequence, the heavy rouge on her cheeks was laid unpredictably and her auburn wig, a flat dish-like affair, was tilted at unexpected angles. Upon the position of this wig, her appearance much depended. Sometimes she would lie back in her chair, her rouged and ravaged face haloed like a saint's; at others, her eyes obscured by this red tam o'shanter, she would seem to stare fixedly at her lap. These metamorphoses and the disorder of her old-fashioned dress – for she was an untidy woman – lent her an air that was comic until you heard her speak. It was a deep masculine voice of great authority. Madame de Chérence lived in a suite of upstairs rooms where Clotilde attended every morning at half-past nine. I never penetrated there, and should hardly have known what the big solitary woman looked like if she had not made occasional appearances on the terrace.

A lift, contrived in one of the many turrets of the house and only large enough to take a wheelchair, connected her rooms with the terrace. On fine evenings in the summer, shortly before sunset, we heard the lift creaking and groaning and a moment or two later she emerged. A manservant would push her chair across the gravel to the balustrade, set a silver bell within reach, and strike a light for one of the long thin cheroots that she had learnt to smoke in Indo-China, a young married woman sixty years earlier. As dusk fell she would sit looking down the smooth channel of parkland that stretched between the forest walls. She often stayed late into the night. Coming in from the woods at dusk and seeing the dull glow of her cheroot on the terrace, we wondered about her childhood and the life she had led in the colonies. Later, waking in the dark, Clotilde would hear – as I did when I stayed at Chérence – the tinkle of a bell, followed by the groaning of the lift as she went up to bed.

The house at Chérence was an extension of the surrounding forest. In obscure corridors, antlers sprouted from the walls, gnarled boughs that might conceivably have put out buds in spring; oak chairs tormented with carving were reminiscent of the twisted roots of trees; the dusty lapis, agate and chalcedony which overlaid huge Spanish cabinets were hardly more curious than the stones to be found below the moss and vegetation in the woods. The drawers in the smoking room, where the brittle eggs of sea-birds and of waders with sad labels – *Pterodroma neglecta, Tringa solitaria solitaria* – rested in beds of cotton wool, were nests no rarer than those to be found a bare fifty yards away. Even the sombre flock wallpapers displayed peony, acanthus and other natural forms, while the rooms with their ogive arches and doorways, their richly plastered and coffered ceilings, gave the impression of bossy caves. Like the forest in the evening, the soundless rooms, with their stained-glass roundels and vaguely ecclesiastical furniture, seemed to collect the darkness.

Nothing in this house was moved. On a Gothic lectern, a double folio – *Festes à l'occasion du Mariage de Madame Louise-Elizabeth et Don Philipe* – was for all the years I knew it open at an engraving of the Temple of Hymen erected on the Pont-Neuf in 1739; the tasselled chairs were placed where they had long ago been useful; in the hall were ranged, conveniently to hand, the hats and caps which had not been worn for many years. It had become uncertain to whom these, and the walking sticks of malacca, ebony and bamboo, with elaborate silver and ivory heads, had belonged. No one but Madame de Chérence could give a name to the persons in the photographs, whose chased and scrolled frames stood on every table. The young, the lovely and the martial were represented there and beside them – without change of emphasis – photographs of thoroughbred horses, collie dogs and a gnu brought from French Equatorial Africa. All were dead, but Clotilde, inventing histories for animals and people, kept them alive a little longer. Only rumour attributed to a great-aunt seven panels of needlework, the task of a lifetime, that reconstructed the legend of Tristram. It was not certain which member of the family had collected the shells that filled three cabinets in the library. These, unlike the birds' eggs, carried both Latin and French names. We blew the dust from them, and heard the sea in the Grand

Nautilus; but the striped *Tigres de Malabar* were silent. My con-
tribution to the mythology of these cabinets was a theory that the
silent shells had come from tideless or semi-tideless seas ('such as the
Mediterranean,' I explained). Various and beautiful, dun, iridescent,
polished as mahogany, wrinkled and veined as a human hand,
whorled or ribbed, smooth or spiky, they aroused our wonder. The
giant clams, we knew, closed on the feet of divers, but there were
other shells, thin as paper, which seemed too fragile to have been
washed in salt seas. A range of sombre black conches that must
have come from stormy coasts we attributed to the Euxine; others,
salmon-pink, to the Red Sea; others, with purplish rims and backs
mottled like turtles, to the shores of New Guinea. The plump yellow
ones, like pats of curled butter, came, as we both happened to know,
from Concarneau. So all the shells were in a sense returned to the sea,
if not precisely to the oceans from which they had come. We saw
them again wet and glistening, washed by ripples on a palm-
fringed shore, or in grottoes where multi-coloured fish cruised
through filtered light, or even where the tongues of Greenland
glaciers thrust into Arctic water.

I had never known a more satisfactory house. None the less, except
in wet weather, it was only our base of operations. What mattered
was the forest. We explored it during three memorable summers,
charting the landmarks, gradually mapping the kingdom. On the day
we first established the position of the heronry, the birds were awaiting us motionless and solemn on their flat airy platforms. They
watched our progress, insect-like, through the underbrush far below.
They saw us gaze up. With a shrug of its hunched grey shoulders, a
sentinel bird pushed off from its nest, like a swimmer thrusting into
water, and slowly circled, skimming the treetops. Returning to its

post, it again reminded us as it dropped its long legs among the topmost boughs of a swimmer feeling for the bottom with outstretched toes. We were always being watched by birds. On one occasion, an autumn evening, our way led across a ploughed field that encroached, like a bay, into the forest. Moving quickly, we had crossed several furrows before we realised that we were observed. Not one but many pairs of eyes fixed and held us. Stationed on the ridges all about, yet camouflaged by the brown soil, were twenty or more long-eared owls. Immobile they had watched our progress. We could only turn and retreat into the wood. They must have been on their autumn migration southward.

Such experiences gave us the certain impression that it was less a matter of our discovering the forest than of the forest arranging our appearances for its own satisfaction. Nowhere was this sense of being watched for and awaited so immediate as in the sunken quarry. It was curious that a quarry should exist near Chérence, for no rock broke surface in that sandy plain. Though the quarry was large it was remote and we stumbled on it by chance. The working had been long abandoned; the raw scar had healed and the forest had returned. The ground sloped imperceptibly into the quarry and we found ourselves with surprise below the level of the surrounding woods. We pushed on wondering, until from a skirt of foliage the curving rock-face rose sheer above us. It offered no passage and as we stood encircled our hushed voices echoed off the cliff. A shallow pool at its base reflected the green of the forest on the quarry lip above. No breeze ruffled this pool however gusty the day. Beside it, we talked in whispers.

Other discoveries, though less dramatic, seemed full of consequence. No one else had found the deserted hives of the charcoal burners, or the impenetrable tangle of raspberry canes that filled the enclosed glade where they grew with a sickly scent. Small objects, like curious flints and etched stones, left us speechless. Peering into the gloom of a hollow tree-trunk we saw the faint glow of two owl's eggs. As though such things were not strange enough, Clotilde endowed the landscape with qualities and features of her own. Some parts of the forest were 'lucky', others 'unlucky', and strict rituals were imposed upon them. Thus an area known as the New Chase was only to be approached through the divided bole of an ash, a freak misshapen growth; while to enter the White Thicket, which to the north of the house stretched as far as the river, it was essential to walk, carefully balancing, down a huge beech trunk that from the edge of the park had crashed into the forest. It was a bridge from the open sunlight into the dark of the wood. Clotilde made a speciality of such things and places, thickets that suddenly unfolded upon an open glade, twisted and unexpected growths, inexplicable moss-covered mounds, vistas that deceived and seemed, by some trick of shape or memory, somewhere else in the wood. There was even a glade, visible only if approached from one direction and at a time of day when the light was favourable, which Clotilde discovered in a folio in the library where the rubric read *Vue dans le forêt de Huelgoat, Finistère*. Once, pointing towards the river, she said, 'Look, the castle!' Through a heat haze, the outlines of the trees shimmered. At first I saw nothing. Then, for a conclusive moment, turrets, battlements and even the standard on the keep were visible.

The forest of Clotilde's imagination acquired authority from a discovery which was not easily explained. One day when I came over from Chantemesle she was tense and preoccupied. For some reason we could not escape Miss Partridge until after tea, and it was late when Clotilde led the way quickly across the park. The shadows went flocking with us, the evening sun throwing our small serious figures into relief. We turned into the forest down a familiar ride, mossy and soundless. Flutes of sunlight slanted through the trees. In the silence we heard the wing-beat of a hawk, and a rabbit's skull, white and brittle, snapped with the crack of a pistol as I trod on it. In a part of the forest that we knew well, Clotilde stopped. After a moment's hesitation, she turned and pressed through the undergrowth. It fought against us, twigs flicking my cheeks and catching in Clotilde's hair. Then suddenly the branches ceased to tug. The green curtains were drawn back. We stood unhampered, in sunlight, on a circle of sward. Two or three hummocks, smooth swellings on the smooth turf, were dotted with rabbit droppings and the rabbits' well-defined paths ran, a darker green, on the grass. A few purple thistles seemed in their secret surroundings rare flowers. Set in this place, its stone coping cushioned in the turf and blotched with orange lichen, was a well. Motes drifted in the sun. The place was complete. Could it always have been there, unknown and unsuspected, in an area so familiar, in a part of the forest so often explored?

We leant on the coping of the well. From the water far below, our reflections, less than life-size, stared at us. If our eyes wandered, it was difficult to find again the point where the upper air-world ended and the water-world began. The dividing line between reality and image was easily lost. Trying to grasp Clotilde's hand – I could see it in reflection gripping the rim of the well – it was my own hand that I unexpectedly touched. Once again I looked at my hands as though they had been those of a stranger, and the feeling that I have already described came strongly upon me. My hands were not the familiar things I knew, nor I myself simply a boy growing, a mould hardening under the pressure of experience. This well, almost on her doorstep, was evidence that in these woods everything was possible, that here imagination would lead wherever we wished, creating battlements by the river or sinking wells in the forest.

As minutes passed, the brightness ebbed from the leaves around us and the circle of sward grew smaller. Dew fell cold on the coping. In the depths of the well we could no longer see our reflections, and the damp air rising from the water roused the skin on our cheeks. Where ferns were clamped below in the crannies of the masonry, a spider jolted from thread to thread. As his netting sagged, it glittered in the dampness. We had to go, but I took with me the inexplicable happiness that is sometimes found in dreams.

 *Seven*

'THESE,' said the old man, leaning forward in the basket chair by the summerhouse, 'are the names of the river's seven mouths:

> *'Pelusiac, Tenetic,*
> *Mendesian, Phatnitic,*
> *Sebennetic,*
> *Canopic and Bolbotine.'*

He intoned the words as if they were verse.

Embayed by the wood, the lawn was a green water; there was the same bird intermittently singing that I had heard as I peered through the bushes on that first expedition. But now I was seated at the garden table beside Clotilde and an exercise book lay open before me. The voice resumed. 'When the Levantine fishermen whose sails are copied from the swallow's wing (no other rig so catches the faintest breeze) take soundings off the Egyptian coast, they bring up on their lines not the gravels of the sea-bottom, but the black silt of Abyssinia, soil that the Nile has brought two thousand miles from the Queen of Sheba's garden.' Neither Monsieur Thibaut – 'Thib' as we called him – nor Clotilde and I regarded this as news of a purely geographical sort. Once again the incantation drifted off into the wood:

> '*Pelusiac, Tenetic,*
> *Mendesian, Phatnitic,*
> *Sebennetic,*
> *Canopic and Bolbotine.*'

It was in my second 'Chérence' summer, when in my parents' absence I was spending a week or two at the house, that Thib became for me, as he had long been for Clotilde, an important person. Three afternoons a week were his. We either sat in the shade by the summerhouse, where birds and rustling leaves were the background to all he told and read, or on special occasions had the forest itself as our schoolroom. Walking down a green tunnel towards a distant eye of light, he told the story of Aucassin and Nicolette, or spoke of sylphs and the metamorphoses of men and women. He moved fast, with a long shambling gait, arms dangling loosely at his sides, and we would break into a trot to keep abreast of him. If it rained we settled in the library. There, perched on neo-Gothic chairs, no sound distracted, unless you cared to imagine the hiss and murmur in the seashells, living their own lives in the mahogany cabinets. My presence at first made Thib uneasy. Only when he found that I was not a rival for Clotilde's attention was I welcomed to the territory of poem, myth and ballad, where he dug like some ageing, gold-drugged prospector. We both listened absorbed to his stories and incantations. They seemed to speak obliquely of our own forest, and to hold the same magic and carry the same exciting promise as our explorations. The names of the classical mouths of the Nile floating into the leaves came naturally to rest on the seven forest rides. Their passage took a bare twenty-four hours. Thib showed us more of our landscape than we had discovered ourselves.

It was not easy to guess his age. Probably he was not as old as we imagined, yet he had been at Chérence longer than anyone could remember, except Madame de Chérence. She had given him a home years earlier. The servants either disregarded or despised him, detecting the smell of indigence. Dirty, gaunt and rheumy, he lived solitary over the stables in a loft that was reached by a quaking wooden stairway. Passing through the stable-yard at any hour of the day or night, you might hear him break into verse. '*Le vieux baragouine toujours,*' the servants said contemptuously. If you crept up the stairs and peered into the room, you saw him pacing up and down as he intoned, on his face a look of worried concentration. Poetry, mythology and medieval romance lay stacked in piles on the floor and on the deal table that occupied the centre of the room. Many of these books he must have read again and again. It was not their apparent content which mattered, any more than the mere layout of the forest was our preoccupation, but some simple yet indecipherable message which they contained. Time and again they led him to the threshold of a discovery for which his whole life had been a search. The image of the lonely prospector recurs; revelation must have seemed only a matter of perseverance.

Stretching out a hand (it would have seemed like ivory had it not been grey with grime), he would pull a book towards him across the table. I can still see the slurred trails his books left in the dust, as if some blind creature had been dragging itself about in his vicinity. There was dust everywhere, even in the folds of his jacket. Behind a curtain in one corner his few clothes hung, and on the hearth, deep in wood ash, stood a large chipped enamel jug. His coffee brew was made to last several days, and inside the jug a series of rings showed, like wrack-levels on a beach, the stages by which the liquid had fallen. A screen, splashed with grease, hid a few pots and pans, but he seemed rarely to eat. Apart from the supply of cheroots which

Chantemesle

Madame de Chérence sent him weekly, his diet was poetry, the thumbed books from which he must have first taken nourishment many years earlier. As far as we could tell he slept in snatches, dossing down on a horsehair couch against the wall. From the moment he closed his eyes, he seemed, in his extreme emaciation, dead. His was a way of life most people would term inhuman, but Clotilde and I gave him our unquestioning allegiance.

In the following year, when I again spent part of my holidays at Chérence and joined once more in Clotilde's lessons, things had changed. Though we were the same trio by the summerhouse, surrounded by the same trees, interrupted by the same birds, a note of urgency was apparent in Thib's voice and manner. As though trying to tear out its heart for us, he avidly broached one poem after another. I had a feeling that we were involved in a conspiracy of which only Thib understood the meaning. He seemed to be conveying information whose sense always escaped us. He would recite with insistence the same passages again and again, as though by dint of repetition a message, quite other than that conveyed in syntax, might reach us. I see him leaning forward in his basket chair, thrusting towards us the elongated head with its shining eyes, like a skull with a candle flickering inside, and I hear the anxiously repeated phrase, 'Do you follow? Do you follow?' As he waited for some response, some sign of an understanding that was not ours, his look showed frustration and pain. It was perhaps to escape from such things that he invaded our forest on long solitary walks. Sometimes we met him. More often, from the thickets where our expeditions led, unseen and in silence we watched him shambling down the rides. One might have expected to hear the rattling of bones as he passed. Occasionally we caught glimpses of him in the far distance, moving

62

fast through open glades where the big trees, that he never saw, sailed steadily past him.

In a year the forest itself had changed. It had grown, and continued to grow daily, more unusual and more subject to the caprice of Clotilde's imagination. Birds previously unknown even at Chérence haunted the leaf-muffled aviaries, the castle reappeared by the river and its life became complex and absorbing, several times we saw Armand on the giant roan posting down a distant ride, and Clotilde reported the appearance of inexplicable reflections in the depth of the well. We hardly knew the paths we walked, or whether the things seen in the glades were fact or fancy. The boundaries of real and unreal disappeared. Clotilde was able to make of the forest anything she wished, in one place creating, in another taking away. We inhabited a stretch of country that bore no resemblance to anything on a map.

The changes in the forest were no doubt partly due to the strain which our lessons began to place upon us. Strange occurrences, the unusual seen or heard, were our unconscious response to the note almost of supplication with which Thib addressed us. One evening, leaning on the coping of the well, exploring the fading reflections through the damp air below, we grew frightened. We were out of our depth. All at once there were too many private sites, too many shapes of our own creation in the woods. We made for the house. In the difficult days that followed we went less into the forest than ever before.

As the summer drew to an end and the first trees, the chestnuts, began to turn, Thib must have felt there was no time to lose. I should soon be going back to school, and Clotilde was starting her first term at a convent near Paris. Next year we should return older, less accessible, perhaps altogether changed. Day by day the pace and strain of our lessons grew more bewildering. The verses and the myths which had delighted us became forbidding. Though Thib never lost patience, never in his frustration set between us his age or his authority, we quietly resisted the pull he was exerting. Sitting on the lawn with my exercise book closed (Thib never asked us now to write anything), sensing an appeal to which I was unable to respond, the same panic seized me as when crossing the river from La Roche, tugging (it seemed vainly) at the heavy oars and dizzied by the glaring light and the water that moved too fast.

We grew to dread our lessons, and soon found ourselves with the cunning of the young replying to his troubled looks and questions with looks and replies that were false. We dared not show how we lagged behind; yet the gap steadily widened between us, a gap created by his very intensity and pain. Unlike the grown-up world and untouched by its preoccupations, he had seemed one with us, yet now he revealed himself inexplicably different. The situation was not easy for us to handle. We could only cheat, and wait.

One day – it must have been about mid-September – Thib announced that we would take our lesson in the forest. For some reason we started late. He strode off at his usual pace but in silence, a silence broken only by odd mutterings. We might not have been present. It was as though, invisible, we accompanied him on one of those solitary walks, moments of which we had glimpsed from thickets or surprised down vistas in the woods. Stumbling after him, we were continually trotting to keep up. Breathless we passed the circle where the seven rides met (' . . . *Canopic and Bolbotine*'), the dank fosse which Armand was said to have jumped on Rosinante, the turning to the charcoal burners' huts, and the giant anthills. Where could we be going? Thib's silence and his mutterings had at first embarrassed us. Now we were frightened. Suddenly, where the path struck off towards the heronry, he wheeled on us and began to shout. Thib had never shouted. The sound of that cracked voice appalled us. 'Get back,' he screamed. 'What are you doing here?' As we hesitated dumbfounded, the old man turned and hurried away. A moment later we were running through the woods. Dusk fell as we reached the house. The motionless shape on the terrace and the glow of Madame de Chérence's cheroot were for once reassuring.

Next morning, after discussion with Clotilde, I sneaked up the rickety wooden stairs to see if Thib was safely back in the stable-loft. I was not halfway up when he called, 'Robin, is that you?' as though expecting my visit. I found him standing dejectedly below the skylight which lit the room. 'Come here,' he said in a voice from which the urgency, but not the pain, had gone. 'I have something for you.' Looking at me with remote affection, he dropped a small object in my palm. I saw a worn silver coin, the size of a half-crown. On one side appeared a shield and something about *Johannes P. Regens*; on the other a Greek cross and the inscription *In Hoc Signo Vinces*. 'It is for that side I give it you. Now please go.'

All the heavy morning, low clouds rode over the forest and rain threatened. In the smoking room, Clotilde and I started relining the cabinet drawers with fresh cotton wool. The birds' eggs lay uneasily in their new nests, and our thoughts were elsewhere. Being so much a part of our myths and of our forest, Thib and his misery involved us deeply. When Clotilde left without a word, I knew she too had gone to the stables. Later, through the windows, I saw her walk across the terrace. She held something cupped in her palms. The secret present, which she never showed me, was locked in a box in her bedroom.

Neither the weather nor the sense of trouble lifted with the afternoon. We lacked the spirit to go out and hung about the house, filled with foreboding. Once again Clotilde left me, abruptly and with an air of determination. She returned bewildered. 'I don't understand what he means,' she said. 'I don't understand.' The evening came at last and in the failing light we made our way down the stone passage hung with antlers to Miss Partridge's sitting-room where we usually had our supper. We went subdued to bed.

I woke to find Clotilde in my room. The night had cleared and a shaft of moonlight fell across the carpet.

'We must go to the forest.'

I stared.

'Get dressed. It's important,' she said. 'It's Thib.'

A minute later we were creeping down the stairs. The night made them unfamiliar; we might have been in a strange house. Feeling our way across the library, we opened one of the long windows. The shutters groaned. Beyond, we stepped into moonlight and tiptoed over the gravelled terrace. A milky light bathed the face of the house and dripped from the pinnacles and balustrades. In this whiteness the windows under their fretted canopies looked like squares of inky serge. Clotilde unhesitating started across the park. The expanse of grass was like a sea, and on its slow rise and fall the trees floated, each tree trailing its shadow like a wake. There was a heavy dew.

The milky light muffled sound and imposed the hush through which we moved. When Clotilde spoke, turning a tense face, her voice sounded like an echo. 'We must hurry,' she said. Leaving the park beyond the New Chase we plunged into the woods. They were nowhere thicker; once off the path we should have been hopelessly lost. The little moonlight that reached us seeped through dense beds of leaf. When we took a yet smaller track, I realised we must be making for the quarry. We followed its dim windings more by sense than sight, our sleeves plucked by bushes, our faces jerking away from the sudden touch of leaves. With arms raised to ward off unseen branches, we made from one obscure gleam of moonlight to another, until dramatically above the trees, as though floodlit, appeared the quarry face. As we drew close, it towered over us, seeming far higher than by day, its planes and angles washed by the white liquid distilling from the sky. The stagnant pool at the rock foot looked like mercury. Disturbed, a dark bird swung from a ledge, tracing a parabola through the breathless air, and floated behind us down the wood. We must have stood a long time staring at the dark fringe of trees on the lip of the quarry. Our feet were wet and our jerseys smeared with dew. We grew cold.

At last the immense silence, the underwater stillness, was broken. A pebble, dislodged from the cliff-top, bounced and clinked into space. The sound scorched and rent the air, spreading in widening circles over the forest. As it died away, we saw, far above, a shaking of leaves and boughs. A moment later, Thib appeared at the precipice edge. With hands outstretched, he stared into the gulf of light, the white tide that drowned the forest. We could make no sound or gesture. Seconds passed before Clotilde stepped forward with a cry. Thib's arms dropped slowly to his sides and slowly his gaze fell from the sky to the forest and then to the patch of moonlit ground where we stood. With a groan that we could hear a hundred feet below, he turned from the brink.

We did not see Thib again. A day or two later Clotilde and I went our different ways to school. When I returned to Chérence in the following summer we had both changed and the forest we had known was no longer there. I found a mere disposition of trees and rides. Only Thib's coin remained a witness to the other demesne we had imperfectly discovered, and which Thib, with his mad and saintly rectitude, was worthy to inhabit. What had he wished us to understand? Perhaps simply that our forest was the real one.

ॐ *Eight*

A<small>S I GREW</small> into adolescence, I could no longer pierce the thin disguise of leaf and twig. The reflections swaying on the river told me little and the valley, that unity of a thousand elements, grew discomposed. A period follows in which the images are blurred. Only Madame Paillard emerges clearly. I have said that Battouflet and I had the hillside to ourselves. This is not strictly true. Madame Paillard, a tall, hazel-eyed woman, with a paralysed hand tucked into the pocket of her linen coat, was a vagrant there. At intervals I had met her with basket and trowel, exploring remote places for the rare plants that grew on the chalk soil. She carried with her an aura, almost a fragrance, of content, and such meetings would distinguish the day from others as surely as if I had been given the sight of an uncommon bird or caught some new aspect of slope and combe.

People regarded Madame Paillard as a mystery, and women spoke almost with resentment of a beauty impervious to time. She must have been over forty when I first remember her. Though she lived alone, she had a visitor each Easter and each August. I saw him more than once, a swart southerner who spoke French with an Austrian accent. Beside him she looked taller and fairer. His visits, I learnt years later, were her true changes of season. They were the return of the sun for which she waited in confidence, and whose warmth lingering through intervening months released the fragrance of which I was aware. It is said that one woman in a thousand still exhales the faint scent of musk, the primitive biological lure, of which evolution has robbed the rest. Perhaps it is the attribute of women like Madame Paillard, who build their lives round a single passion. Hers, heroic and illogical, lasted twenty years. Existence for most people is shaped on the one hand by a sober domesticity or despairing dissipation, on the other by considerations of money, power or repute. Living by the private calendar of imagination and passion, she knew nothing of these.

Her life, her real life, had begun on a picnic in the Bregenzerwald when she was a young widow, and he a young married man dressed in ridiculous leather shorts and a green hat with a *Gemsbart*. Leaving the party they had wandered upward among rocks and pines. After the morning's rain their feet made no sound on the sodden pine needles. Those who watched them go saw two figures among the trees barred by shafts of sunlight, now their heads illuminated, now their bodies; then they passed out of sight. An hour later, a jay scolding in the branches halted them; they felt an unsuspected breeze and heard somewhere the cluck of running water. Turning to each other, they found a third presence under the pines, a relationship already complete, as though born in full emotional panoply, sprung there like Athene armoured from the head of Zeus. They had little to say, for it seemed that everything had been said; but they returned with a talisman against disaster. In the wood, they had floated off on a current other than the muddy Mississippi of time. The visits began in the following year. Certain as the return of the seasons, they continued until his death. It was no wonder that Madame Paillard seemed content to find rare orchids on the hillsides; no wonder, as I like to think, that she carried a fragrance of musk. Presences found in the Bregenzerwald, or anywhere, are rarely so impervious to time.

After one of our chance meetings on the hillside, Madame Paillard asked me to tea. She lived in the nearest upland village. From the cloud-reflecting lake where my father fished, the roofs were visible beyond the corn. I knew her house. Through iron gates which no longer closed, it was approached up a gat-toothed avenue of Spanish chestnuts. Young trees fenced against cattle replaced the giants that had fallen. Pear trees were trained *en espalier* against the front of the house and farm buildings rose behind. Geese and a sense of husbandry reached the back door. A pond filmed with duckweed lay on the edge of the formal garden. Its far bank was cattle-muddied and reed-fringed, recalling the casual ponds that were a feature of the upland villages. At one end of the house rose a ruinous tower with a cartouche over the door. Swallows entering the unglazed windows had taken possession – no doubt the same swallows as dipped on the lake – and the winding stairs were littered with straw and stained with droppings.

I found Madame Paillard between box hedges that radiated from a paved terrace on one side of the house. She carried a shallow wicker basket, half-filled with the withered roses that she had been cutting. Her smile of welcome set me at ease and gave me comfort. In her presence I found a sense of enveloping warmth, tinged with inexplicable excitement. For tea we sat at one end of the stone-flagged hall, the coolest room in summer, and she led me to talk of Chantemesle and the river. The house was very quiet.

It was the first of many visits. In the same cool room or sitting on the terrace, she told me of the rare flowers on the *côte*, some of them growing tamed in her garden. I told her of the birds. She spoke also of Austria, of the pinewoods, dark on the sunniest days, of the gleaming scarves of snow and the peaks that in midsummer seemed to lie a stone's throw from the trees but were two or three long hours above. As I later remembered, she also mentioned a niece, Michèle, whom she wished me to meet. As it turned out, our first meeting was still three or four years distant. Meanwhile, I worshipped Madame Paillard. Her charm that was like a scent and the fact that she was of the hillside, a friend of Battouflet's who almost shared the landscape, made it inevitable. I thought of her often, wondered about her solitary life and dreamt that she might ask me to come and live with her. In the hope of meeting, I deserted the river even in high summer and spent hours on the *côte* waiting for her rare appearances. The time came when I began to turn up at her house uninvited, at first with some flower that I hoped would interest her and later with no pretext at all. My devotion must have grown an embarrassment, for invitations came less frequently and firmly though gently she set a distance between us. For a time I was puzzled, as though some sleight of hand had taken place. I retreated for comfort to Battouflet. He was pleased. My reports on the hillside had long been desultory.

When I next see Chantemesle clearly, time has passed and a change of lighting has occurred. To the brilliance of childhood mornings, to motionless midday and to the haze of afternoon, moonlight has succeeded. A long summer night has fallen on river and hillside. Unlike a sleepless man who longs through the darkness for the coming day, his proper element, I longed at midday for the night landscape, my meridian. I carried within me the phases of the moon, knew at luncheon whether it waxed or waned, and which planets would be visible after sunset. The Chantemesle nights developed an individuality that nights have since lacked. Those that were overcast engulfed me. On the hillside nothing was visible but an easing of the darkness at the skyline and a hint of grey where the chalk bluffs rose. I moved by touch along the paths. By contrast, the nights of high cirrus diffused a watery radiance that was deceptive. They annihilated sense of distance. I stretched a hand to the nectarine on the wall or the smooth bole of the catalpa to find them a dozen feet away.

The nights when the moon rose free above the valley were dazzling brilliance. In this light, tree-shadows were darker than their trees; each cottage bordered a pool of jet; and the rim of the standing corn was bounded by a black trench. My own shadow blotted out the grass at my feet. Patterns appeared, discernible at no other time, and the relationship of a tree to a barn, or of a path to the orchard it crossed, was inexplicably transformed. Sounds and movements were intensified: a poplar leaf burned as it eddied earthward; crazed frogs on the islands deafened me; the trembling of a spider's web shook the valley; a hare slipping through the corn made a tumult; and a wispy breeze, approaching undetected and passing as suddenly, fell on the trees like a hurricane. Since it seemed that the graceless motion of my hand would disturb the light, I moved on such nights more exposed and more circumspectly than at midday. Sometimes, as I searched for an adequate response, the moon slid behind a rising bank of cloud and I was released anonymous and unchallenged.

A second shadow falls beside mine on the grass. There is moonlight on a dress, and a bare arm pushes aside the branches. A face bends over flowers (all the flowers are white in the night landscape) and a voice says, 'The quiet under the trees, the drifts of moonlight . . . ' Sometimes we launch a canoe on black silk, silk that rustles and is alive. Touching it with our fingers as it draws us between the islands, we are surprised to find it wet. Sometimes we go through the fields without a word. Our footsteps crushing the curded grass leave a single track, for our feet like our thoughts move together and our hands are clasped. Sometimes we scramble up the hillside. Luminous above the copses, the chalk bluffs like bland moons seem a second source of light. On the hilltop we lean against the wind as it flows across the Île de France and see the shining arms of the river far below. We hear the calls of migrating birds, some no higher above the valley than we are. Their signals are part of a mystery we share. There is no separation between us and all things living.

Cranach painted her, long-thighed, the small high breasts, the sensitive heart-shaped face turned slightly to one side and in the eyes a look both of detachment and surprised inquiry. There is a balance of mind and limb, a stillness too still but for the smile and a body whose touching beauty seems to speak of the fate of all bodies.

✳ Nine

I MET Michèle on a still August evening at Les Grands Prés, the house near which I had first seen Clovis when I lost my way as a boy on the upland. In the intervening years the house had grown familiar as one of several where a group of us from the surrounding countryside gathered at the parties that were a feature of the late summer. We gathered with repeated expectation and pleasure, and we seemed, because we were much of an age, to have much in common. Time, emphasising differences of bent and character, proved the impression wrong. We merely shared the youth we have all lost, and most of us now have little to say to one another. Yet, as I look back on those friends, hear our laughter and our solemn conversations, and recall the sense of standing confidently on the threshold of experience, I feel affection. I see Clotilde, without her ties and dinner-jackets; Dedette, like a beautiful and audacious bird, without her seven children; Edouard, without the dukedom and the acres that have engulfed him; Jean-Pierre, before his glitter was dimmed in a sea of drink; and Antoine, before he followed the *Croix de Lorraine* to chilling eminence. At this remove I can even accept Clovis.

Les Grands Prés was a pure example of the Empire style. The

Napoleonic contractor who built it, Clovis's great-grandfather, had furnished the house about 1810 in one sumptuous stroke. It remained unaltered, and Clovis had been rocked in an Empire cradle. The bias of the provincial nobility, whose houses mainly dated from an earlier century, led some to view the upstarts at Les Grands Prés with reserve. Even then I wondered why my mercantile origin escaped censure: perhaps because I was a foreigner and my parents were not rich. The sophisticated owners of Les Grands Prés were wealthy enough to attract envy and criticism.

We, the young, were critical chiefly of the unresilient marble floor on which we danced. Yet the hall had its compensations. Pier-glasses hung on walls of faded yellow silk, and between the glasses stood, on alabaster columns, urns alternately of malachite and jasper. Giltwood consoles topped with travertine and, in the window embrasures, Grecian settees, upholstered in the same faded silk as the walls, were the only furniture. At one end of the hall the sequence of silk and glass was interrupted by an enormous picture, heroic in theme and scale. Revealing here a muscled thigh and there a swelling breast, noble Romans, dwarfing the dancers below, were fixed in neo-classic splendour: the suppliant forever on bended knee, the hero superbly remote, the legionaries attentive, the matrons confident in their Republican virtue. From an altar, carved with rams' heads, rose a wisp of sacrificial smoke.

When poorer neighbours were hurrying to install electricity and ruining the appearance of their houses, Clovis's parents could afford the affectation of candles. Reflected in the pier-glasses, these candles were repeated in other halls that stretched with their dancers into shadowy distance, into other parties and other evenings. Their light caught the ormolu rims of the urns, the cuirass of the handsome centurion standing at the hero's elbow, the white arms of the suppliant and the whiter bosoms of the matrons. Though the candles raised a glow on the waxed marble floor, they left pools and corners of obscurity which extended the hall as did its mirrored reflections. From a light, soft as gold, the dancers passed into enclaves of gloom and were lost. They emerged unconscious of their absence, yet seemed as though returned from private journeys. Clotilde preoccupied, Dedette with a laugh cool as a thrush, would circle with their partners into the aura of the candles and seem like guests newly arrived.

Michèle appeared in one of the long glasses, a face seen over a shoulder, a face first noticed merely as unfamiliar. As she danced with Clovis, her face recurred, smaller yet clearer, moving in another mimic hall. I began to look for it among the faces about me, but found it always distant, in the mirrors or fading into the bower-like glooms. Once I sensed it signalled. There was no smile, or that softening of feature, as though a mind were brushed by tenderness, that later linked us across a crowded room. It was simply as if she had seen someone she thought she knew, but had realised her mistake before it found expression.

Waltzing with Clotilde, I felt that the face was no longer among the dancers or in the mirrors. Drawing away from the candlelight, I searched the eddies and shadows. Peering over Clotilde's shoulder, I saw beside a darker head a brushstroke of honey-coloured hair. But it was only Dedette with one of her sighing lovers.

'What's the matter?' Clotilde said. 'Are you looking for someone?'

'Who should I be looking for?' I answered. 'Let's go into the garden.'

The dew was damp underfoot. Though the trees on either side of the lawn were like dark cumuli, clouds repeating on a vaster scale the bowers of the hall, a thin summer light, sensed rather than seen, lingered in the sky. It seemed to ennoble the figures standing there and made them loom large as the statues on their plinths. I recognised the suppliant beside Dedette, Antoine the chill and dedicated hero, Edouard the patrician senator. Jean-Pierre, glass in hand, slipping from us, was already on the borders of his private world.

Voices on the lawn were indistinct, an echo of the murmur that must have hung earlier that hot August day over the surrounding fields. Yet as we passed our friends, their figures at the same time shadowy and imposing, a phrase would detach itself, as though the night air gave it roundness. The stone statues might have been pronouncing oracles. I alone seemed to give off no ring. A footman bore down with a tray of glasses, his gloves in the gloom strangely white. Approaching the stream we heard it hustling by. Swans, immaculate as the footman's gloves, lumbered on the grass. Clovis, to the accompaniment of inane laughter, was feeding them ladies' fingers dipped in champagne. My evening seemed at an end.

As I returned to the house, I found her on the steps; not a face, but a silhouette outlined against the glow from the open doors. I took her in to dance. As a boy who has stepped up and received a school prize dares not look at it, so I dared not look at her in the candlelight, but searched for her reflection in the mirrors. There I saw our heads together and in dimmer halls her straight hair floating past dimmer urns and seeming, though colours were uncertain, the colour of alabaster. We looked at each other only in the eddies and bowers of shadow, seeming then to search in blurred features for the thing that drew us together. As we circled back to the glow of the candles, and light redefined cheek-bone and chin, we dropped our eyes.

Later, we met again the summer murmur rising from the lawn. Figures were statues; a pair of gloves, like lights, traced an erratic orbit; a white dress burnt. By the stream there was a glow, perhaps swans, or could it be white hydrangeas. We turned into the cloud-bank of trees, whose tops described huge curves against the sky. 'I will show you the temple,' I said. From the lawn a swathe of rougher grass led between towering shapes. The temple, blotted against the wood, came as a surprise: we saw it almost as we touched the pillars. A classical folly, once the pleasure of Napoleon's contractor, it smelt of damp and ferns, as though the stone had become vegetable. On the steps, leaning against the pillars, our straying hands met and once more we stared at each other in surprised question.

As time passed, an indefinable change came over the wood. Though there was no wind, the trees stirred and drew our eyes to their rounded tops. Their curves seemed more sharply drawn, with a hint of individual leaf and twig. At last, like real clouds they became tipped with silver, and at the same time the lawn beyond lit up like a distant stage, its spaces studded with statues and people that threw shadows. The moon had risen. Though it had not reached us, its snow drifted across the lawn, mantling Edouard's ample shoulders, falling whiter than white on Dedette's dress. As though to shake themselves free, the figures began to move, taking their shadows with them. Crossing and recrossing the visible strip of lawn, they grew steadily brighter.

A wedge of moonlight now fell diagonally across the far end of the rougher grass that led to the temple. To one side, all was still dark, but on the other glistering foliage, armfuls of leaves, appeared where before had been only cumuli. The light, like driven snow, was carried into the boughs, gathering in drifts on outspread branches, penetrating here and there even to the trunks and piling knee-deep on the ground below. As we watched, the moon lifted from the stencil of leaves above the farthest trees and its slanting rays, at first smoky as mist, explored the channel before us. They touched the leaden dome of the temple, crept down the pillars to where we stood and shone on the drenched grass at our feet.

The light troubled us as it had troubled the figures on the lawn. We turned into the wood, whose dark wall had now become individual trees rising among snowdrifts. In clearings that the gardeners never reached, hummocks of bramble cupped the snow-light in their curled leaves or caught it like frost along the leaf edges. We moved through the windless blizzard, picking our way from drift to drift, and sometimes in the white spaces we stopped, seeing this snow settle on clasped hands as easily as it settled on the grass.

We had long lost the murmur from the lawn, when in the silence we heard a scuffling at our feet. The air held the sound after it ceased. We listened: again the scuffling and again silence carrying the echo of the sound. Then we saw, half in snow-grass, half in bramble-shadow, something twisting, the caricature of a rabbit. The snare had tightened through the fur into the flesh. I knelt on the wet grass. The rabbit lay as though stunned, but each time I tried to ease the noose it gave a jerk, tearing at the grass with its paws. As I fumbled and she hung over me, there was another sound. A twig snapped, someone stepped from the snowless depths of a beech. 'What *are* you up to?' Clovis said. I recalled his appearance years earlier on the edge of the trees beside the river, and how I had briefly backed away. 'Let me do it,' he said. In a moment the snare was off. He held the twitching rabbit by the hindlegs and giving it a sharp blow with the side of his hand (a hand that was still too large) broke its neck. 'It would have died anyway,' he said.

We walked back to the house. The lawn was empty but for the statues and their shadows. In the hall Jean-Pierre, swaying slightly, held a last group with the shining talk that led to nothing. The party at Les Grands Prés was over.

❧ Ten

I ARRIVED at Madame Paillard's two days after the party at Les Grands Prés. It was past four as I hurried along the track that led from the crest of the hillside. There were the usual cornflowers, scabious and poppies; the usual family of partridges crept over the stubble with hunched shoulders; on the horizons the spires moved and beckoned; clouds with curled fronts like white prows drifted on the upland currents. As I turned between the gate-piers I saw under the chestnuts Clovis's gleaming motor, the Voisin *décapotable* that we all envied. It seemed an ill omen, but Madame Paillard met me at the door and on the terrace I found Michèle and the reassurance of friends, Clotilde, Dedette, Edouard and Jean-Pierre. As Michèle and I stood a little apart, red admiral butterflies opened and closed their wings on a towering buddleia. Their brilliance dulled the mauve flowers. The air was charged with the smell of box.

During tea someone stumbled on the uneven paving of the terrace – I hardly realised that it was Clovis – and jogged my elbow. Tea slopped down my new trousers; my cup fell and broke. The following days brought other misadventures. At Dedette's, three strings inexplicably snapped in my tennis racquet; the motor cars one evening left for a picnic without me ('But Clovis said he saw you in the car in front'); hurrying home by twilight from Michèle's I fell headlong over a tripwire, where the path wound steeply down the hillside, and sprained a wrist; a telephone message lured me uninvited to luncheon with Monsieur de M, an ageing *precisian* with the most formal establishment in the valley.

Clovis dogged me with desperation. It was his strategy that Michèle and I should never be alone. One afternoon at her aunt's, while the others were dancing to a gramophone in the drawing-room, we escaped. Rain had fallen earlier in the day, welcome in that August. The butterflies stretched their wings on the refreshed buddleia and swallows banked so low one might have knocked them down. Our footsteps made no sound on the shorn grass between the box hedges. They were tall as a man, and at the end of each walk stood a statue. The stone figures were lodged in niches of green; only a gesturing arm, a trident or a nymph's lichened bosom caught the sunlight. We had hardly reached the basin of water which lay at the foot of Neptune when we saw Clovis following us. As he approached, a voice from the distant terrace called, 'Telephone.' Michèle left with a glance and we were alone. As we confronted each other, I heard the faint notes of the gramophone and the nearer rush of the swallows' wings. The smell of the damp box had grown oppressive.

Casual yet provocative, Clovis considered the pool, and then stepped deliberately on the stone coping. With a glance at me, he judged the distance to the statue and jumped. He landed safely on the far rim. Balancing his way along the edge of the basin, he rejoined me with a look of satisfaction.

'Come on, your turn,' he said.

Though slighter, I was taller and longer in the leg. I stepped on the coping and gathered myself for the jump.

'Go on,' he said.

I could sense him close behind me. As I launched, he gave a brief push that might have masqueraded as encouragement; but it threw me off balance and I missed a footing. Landing in the water, I fell forward and struck the statue. Putting my hand to my face, I found it sticky with blood. Eight feet away Clovis stood watching, his large hands at his sides, his lips moist. The handsome head, the over-solid torso, the short legs, seemed to fill the perspective between the box hedges. I edged back along the rim of the basin.

I hit him with my left and his head jerked back. Then he came at me swinging and I gave ground. As we fought and the swallows threaded effortlessly above, our faces were reddened with the blood running down my cheek. Our fight might have been some perverted blood-pact. Soon we were both panting and through his gasps Clovis began to mutter, talking to himself. I found this hopeful. I was in the centre of the walk, well away from the hedges, and I heard the refrain of the battered old man who had taught me: 'Jab him and leave him, jab him and leave him . . . like a cobra, like a cobra.' At last I jabbed him properly and he hung dazed against the hedge. I thought with relief that it was over. Sorry for us both, I could no longer understand why I was hitting him. He looked at me, still muttering. Then hands down, eyes down, he swayed and dived despairingly at my waist. We fell together, our heads buried in the box. On top of me, he pinioned my arms. Without regard for himself he began to bang his head against mine.

So Michèle and Clotilde found us, bloody as March hares. When we struggled to our feet, I dared not look at them. With amazement I heard Michèle saying – the voice seemed like an oracle but far away – 'That's enough, Clovis; you'd better go before my aunt sees you.' 'Badger,' added Clotilde quietly, who had never liked him. He walked away between the solid hedges and three feet beneath the swallows;

we heard the whirr of his self-starter on the avenue. In the flower-room Michèle washed my face. The end of summer was all mine.

I took her to see Battouflet. It was part of her introduction to the valley. Though he had aged and his hectic songs were rarer, he had lost no edge. With Marguerite, now arthritic like himself, he was sitting in the sun, throned on one of the pleasant pauses which the hillside made in its descent.

'I have heard her voice,' he said.

'Whose voice?' I asked.

'There are not many on the *côte* . . . Come here,' he said to her. She stooped and I thought he was going to touch her face; but perhaps changing his mind he grasped her hand and felt the skin with his thumb as a jeweller appraises a stone.

'This,' he rasped after a moment, showing the valley with a gesture, 'is now yours, I suppose.'

As we went down the hill, he broke into song, a ribald song that followed us faintly to the house.

We walked under the summer's branches, we were wrapped in its green cocoon. Standing in dense copses we seemed like trees, leaves sprouting from our lips and ears, boughs interlacing with our limbs. 'The tree has entered my hands. The sap has ascended my arms.' Foliage on the islands enclosed our single body and the bracken in combes protected us. We left flattened grass and empty forms where we had lain. Though I brushed her skirt and she my jacket we carried home spears of grass, seeds caught in wool and on her blouse the stain of dead insects and threads of crushed antennae. Some of these fragments must survive as dust in corners of the Breton *armoire* where my clothes hung. This seems right. The summer still exists in all its detail – the prick of the thistles, thyme mixing with her breath, birch boughs moving like fingers above us, and the juicy acrid smell of the islands – but Michèle herself is hard to find. When I later met the scent she used, it recalled not a girl but swaying leaves. Her face is now part of the whiteness of moonlight nights, and her breasts are the river silk. Our love was a feature of the local ecology and, though transfiguring, the landscape was part of it. If Michèle for a time brought me closer to the valley, made me see and feel it more fully, breathe it more deeply, the intoxicating weed I had eaten was not native to Chantemesle. The growth was common and its range was wide.

❦ Eleven

I RETURNED to Chantemesle for Christmas. From the affectations and the compromise that now beset me elsewhere, it always seemed a return to myself. 'I have come back to reality': such phrases recur in my diary. Yet on this occasion when I caught the first glimpse of the chalk bluffs from the train beyond Vernon, the feeling of release, of slipping a useless burden, came less readily.

In the afternoon I walked up the *côte* for reassurance. All was as it should have been in winter. The birds were silent. The raw slopes wore their retracted look. With the green gone, the soil-flesh, the substance of the hill, was apparent. Through this naked flesh the bluffs thrust like bones, shoulder-blade and elbow. The denuded spinneys were dank, branches and boles wet with a cold sweat. Moisture gathered at the ends of twigs and pattered to the ground; my jacket was splashed with huge tears. In the valley below, the air was visible as a thin smoke or bluish gruel, whose upper surface lay three hundred feet above the water. White streaks appeared on the river, reflecting gaps in the clouds, and then were gone. The islands, like the *côte*, revealed their essential shapes, soil and leaf-mould under dripping trees. The blue canoe was invisible in the boathouse. I watched a flight of rooks make purposefully over the Firmin villa and settle beyond the river. I was deep in the landscape again.

Michèle arrived at her aunt's soon after Christmas. As she walked down the *côte*, a small shape in the large afternoon, it was part of the landscape coming to meet me. Though the green rooms we had shared were now unfurnished, they still seemed ours. Wandering along the hillside under a smoky sky, we were private as in the leaf-depths. When the sun broke through, and a patch of light travelled from combe to combe, briefly colouring grass and spinney, we stood for a moment in a luminous alcove, a warmth prepared for us in the grey day. It was dusk before we gained the valley road. From a barn we caught the spiced smell of milk and hay. In the light of a lantern, the stalled cows, twenty or thirty of them, looked enormous, and their tossing heads flung shadows among the rafters. With white plumes rising from their nostrils, they were not recognisably the dull Friesians that pastured in the meadows. As we walked home, I watched the sky slowly clear. Stars appeared over the river to the west and the air took a new edge. In the silence, Michèle suddenly said, 'I wonder if you ever look at me as closely as you look at the valley.'

Next day I found a thrush stiff on the lawn, its matchstick legs fending the air. The frost had started. As its grip tightened and the hillside turned to board, as stacks of beet set solid and the plough grew nobbly on the upland, I quickened. The constriction of the cold forced my energies as through a jet. I breathed deeper, and now I too had plumes issuing from my nostrils. As frost patterns glazed the village windows, I saw only more clearly. Drinking the thin sun, I gave off a ring like ice.

In the mornings, as I climbed the frosted hillside to find Michèle, each leaf-blade was cased in icing. The brilliance dulled the chalk bluffs. Though the sun soon melted the rime on the south-facing slopes, the combes remained white all day; so I sometimes passed at a step from hoary spikes into watery green, from winter to a foretaste of spring. Below me, the valley was blue and gold, mist and sun. Shafts of sunlight speared and split the blue above the river. As I returned in the evenings the air seemed about to crack with the cold. The west was apple-green and black branches lay across it. I had a feeling that the planet ceased to turn.

Soon the upland lake was safe for skating. We tried it cautiously. The ice groaned and cracks raced across it; but it held. It was ours alone. We were attended only by magpies, brilliantly black and white, that flopped in thorn trees and by wagtails that walked delicately on the cold glass. Pushing out from the entombed reeds to the dark centre of the lake, we skated for hours and days. Even more than in summer the upland was the crown of the world. With no bellying clouds above, no waist-depth of corn, no larks measuring the air, it was an emptiness that barely knew gravity. Striking out we might have skated over the village spires; we might have fallen off the Île de France.

Our grinding skates scored the lake in wide parabolas that met and parted, yet always returned to the fixed point of ourselves. I would unravel the white lines on the ice, the weals with raised edges, and trace our meeting tracks. Sometimes we skated hand in hand, swinging together, close to each other and to the landscape as in the cocoon of summer. As I look back, the plumes of breath that we trail carry texts, ribbons with words as in comic papers. But they carry, as my head carried, tags of verse. As I sweep across the ice I am followed by 'Lutes, laurels, seas of milk, and ships of amber', and the fluttering ribbons speak of Dido's 'silver arms' and 'The pastures of the firie steeds that draw the golden Sunne'.

Night obscures the texts that must have followed us, the symposium that must have streamed from our lips on the evening of the fancy-dress party. Even Clovis was invited at Michèle's suggestion and came from Paris with new-fangled racing skates. Michèle and I, a shepherdess and pirate, arrived soon after dark. Her dress was white and I wore white linen trousers, for so (I said) we should not lose each other. While Luca and Ada, our Italian servants, built a bristling fire on the bank and hung soup above it in a huge cauldron, we skated down the lake with armfuls of Chinese lanterns and hung them from thorn trees and willows. Each time Michèle struck a match, bare branches and the oval of her face appeared beside me. The night, like all that frozen fortnight, was windless and the candles burnt without a flicker. As she closed the paper lanterns and lifted her arms to the boughs, her face changed to gold or rose. Then moving into the darkness it was lost until the next match spluttered. At the lake-head where a stream still trickled into a pocket of open water, duck rose with a clatter. We heard the thudding of their wings as they banked above us.

When the lanterns were set, we raced up the lake, and on each side of us, as though newly risen, hung Chinese moons, red, white, ochre and amethyst. There was no sound but the thin scraping of our skates. In the distance a white cloth drew us to where they had set on the ice a trestle table, with mousse of chicken and of ham and a dish of Ada's hare *pâté*. Alone, we opened the first bottle of champagne and glass in hand hobbled on our skates up the bank to the blazing fire. We heard voices floating across the iron fields long before our friends materialised suddenly in the orbit of the firelight: nodding ostrich plumes where Dedette came with a Capuchin that was Antoine; Clotilde alone, throwing a long shadow as Mephistopheles; Edouard, noble in silk breeches, sporting the ribbon of the Saint-Esprit; and Jean-Pierre, with his jester's bladder and his wit crackling in the cold. Others followed; and with them Clovis, overdressed as an officer of the Imperial Guard. Clumsy as auks while they stumbled down the bank, on the ice they were released. They glided off, not the fallible friends I knew, but personifications of their costumes – Beauty and Renunciation, Sin, Valour and Jest. The ice carried essences, not people.

Something unconscious as migration drew them down the lake between the lanterns. They were carried as on a breeze. Their common impulse spent, they scattered, mostly two by two, and no orrery could have determined their swoops and circuits. The lake hummed like a tuning fork. Some drained their glasses, some escaping the lantern light drifted in embrace under the private willows, some hissed like meteors down the ice, and some, the expert skaters, watched the long smooth scars they left behind them. Converging and effortlessly parting, they were near and a moment later far away. I saw a white skirt come and go, ostrich plumes caressing a Capuchin's hood, a statesman breasting the moon, Clotilde on the arc of a long circle and Jean-Pierre curvetting with an opened bottle of Ruinart 1923.

The vintage was exhausted years ago, and the skaters now are middle-aged; yet for a moment they seemed timeless, as permanent as the valley and the upland. My vision, as though sharpened by the diffused light and the still air, set these friends on the lake for ever. With them, symbol of another world where time was everything, an officer of the Imperial Guard struck out on racing skates.

It must have been an hour or two later that the lake slowly brightened. Eclipsing the lanterns, the true moon was rising. As I watched, thorn trees and willows took shape along the banks and shone. The ice shone. By comparison with this naked winter moon, the summer nights of the valley seemed overblown. Once more, and almost for the last time, the moon spoke clearly, a Rosetta message revealing what lay in the copses, in the depths of the islands, what Clotilde and I had pursued in the forest. Yet the unexpected clarity of the message, coming almost as a surprise, told me that I was less constantly within the landscape than I had once been and that because of the hug of experience I should not much longer have entry into its timelessness. 'May I be unhappy, lonely and poor,' I said vainly and in silence, 'but may this understanding never leave me.'

As I stood there, the clock in the nearest village struck the hour. One church after another took it up, the sounds coming through the air from great distances, yet fixing the position of each village more precisely than did the wandering spires by day. The passing notes left a deadly unease, a sense that I was being carried away on some unwelcome current from upland, hill and river. In the succeeding silence the timeless landscape broke its mould.

Turning I saw Battouflet beside the dying fire. He held a glass in one hand. With the other he grasped his stick and runnels of moonlight ran down it as he carved the air; Marguerite, with only a month or two to live, sat dozing but safe on the far side of the embers. The sense which often seemed to tell him of my whereabouts had brought him up the hill at midnight. I crunched over the frozen reeds to the lakeside, glad that he had come on this particular evening.

'How is it here now?' he said. I told him that the moon was up and that no moon had been brighter; that the ice was eight inches thick. 'And who is skating?' he said. As he turned sharply to the lake, the moonlight burnt on the rim of his straw hat. Most of the lanterns had gone out and the ice was almost deserted. 'Only one or two left,' I said, and saw far down the lake some friends of Michèle's, Parisians whom I hardly knew. Like the silhouettes of birds crossing the moon itself, they crossed as they skated the path where the moon's reflection fell. Farther still, on the arm of an officer of the Guard I saw a shepherdess in white. 'The last time they skated here was twenty years ago. It hasn't changed,' he said. I refilled his glass and we looked, each in his own fashion, down the lake. The white dress beside the officer was moving very slowly; it drifted to a stop. Battouflet sniffed the air. 'A thaw is coming,' he said.

It arrived twenty-four hours later, and with it the rain. The hillside sagged that had been tense and clear. The copses wept and after a wind the poplars round our house were ankle-deep in the twigs and boughs that they had dropped. Below the house, the meadows squelched and despaired. The islands crumbled, gobbets of soil plopped into the river, and the island trees, losing their shape, hung flaccid over the water. The river itself, instead of drawing with purpose down the valley, showed as mere shreds of light and surface gleams. Determination and personality deserted the landscape, as though the will were tired that had sustained it unbreached against the frost.

Looking out at the valley under drooping cloud, one long afternoon I waited for Michèle. She had gone to tea at Les Grands Prés instead. She left for Paris a day or two later. I wrote in my diary: 'Seeing that life is so short, one ought to be able to be faithful.' And again: 'I saw a flight of plover this morning, curving and stooping across the upland; her house beyond. For birds at least, wing beat and heartbeat, motion and desire, are the same.' Even the valley seemed involved in her defection, as though it also had suffered loss. I found no reassurance where assurance had always been.

❦ Twelve

JULY brought me again to Chantemesle, and once more I found green summer risen in the valley. It had drowned the islands and the meadows; it had swirled round the poplars that trembled in its current; it had hidden the polished arms of the catalpa. Leaf-foam splashed through open windows, and the light in the drawing-room was like light under water. Submerging the house, the tide had edged up the terraces. It floated the apricot trees in the orchard; it lapped round the base of the bluffs. We lay hundreds of feet under summer.

But the summer differed from those I had known. Though Michèle came only once to the valley, I missed her less than I expected. Other voices were striking up and the moonlight fell on other faces. Ideas and manners, alien yet compelling, swept down the river from the capital. The pastoral poets who had shared the combes, and seemed to have been born there, were ousted by lesser names from Paris. Entering the salon of my mother's old friend at Gasny, which had always seemed silent, I was deafened by the talk of an explorer and a man with a large pearl in his tie who made machine-guns; from a house reflected in the river near Vétheuil, untenanted as long as I could remember, issued surprising scents, silks, and women to walk on the lawns; over at Le Pavillon, senators and writers moved to Edith

Wharton's sophisticated measures. On every side phrases and gestures compelled attention where before had been leaves or river. The landscape grew crowded; people were taller than the trees. In the rooms where the summer air stirred the curtains, strangers passed, interrupting the passage of the bees, breaking the patterns of the lace-light on the ceiling. They stubbed out cigarettes in the lavender and rose-petals. Arriving in motor boats, they landed at the boathouse, having never landed on the islands. Arriving in motor cars, they left without exploring the *côte*. 'Where have these people come from?' I said to Clotilde; 'There's an invasion.' 'They have always been here,' she replied. 'We are growing up.'

The worrying sense that I was being drawn away from myself took me to the inn on the outskirts of the hamlet where Battouflet often drank in the evenings. I was glad to sit opposite him; he had no regard for the complicated world of people that was exerting its pull upon me. He belonged to the hillside. As we talked or were silent I could see it through the window beyond the chestnut trees that lined the yard.

The inn was the least attractive building in the hamlet. The creeper that softened the cement-stucco front did not hide a roof of corrugated iron. The interior was bare and non-committal, and its marble-topped tables offered little invitation. On one wall hung a reproduction sanguine of a small boy pissing into a duck pond above the legend *Vaut mieux ne pas boire de l'eau*. In a corner stood a gramophone with a cumbrous horn and a handle that was wound to evoke music when strangers entered. They rarely did except on Sundays. Then jolly men, with blondes plump as the quails they ate, drove for luncheon from Paris. Jean the Basque proprietor was a remarkable cook.

It was Chez Jean that I had first noted the tone of wise men ordering *râble de lièvre* and *daube de Béarn,* and heard chanted the litany of sauces, Béarnaise, Genevoise, Nivernoise, Joinville. Chez Jean also that I had first paid for drinks: a Pernod for Battouflet and for me grenadine and Seltzer with a curl of lemon peel. It was there that I now discovered the comfort of wine. I cannot look back on the discovery with anything but gratitude. Since then I have owed much to the kindest of drugs: women transfigured, landscapes illuminated, days and nights redeemed from gloom and boredom. In moments of despair, there is always help in the thought of the basking vineyards of the world, the sheer number of vines: the fretted slope stretching southward from Dijon, the vines of Tuscany that trail rococo festoons above growing corn and clamber into olive trees, the regimented battalions of the Rhine, the green waves that break on the rocky escarpments of the Katharinenkirche at Sion, Chilean grapes ripening in view of snowcapped volcanoes, the heady must fermenting at the Cape, and on the fringes of fanatic Arabia vines planted in hidden *wadis* by clandestine drinkers. The ordered ranks encircle the world.

The sap is always rising in some continent, and the sticky tendrils feel their way into the sun. At every moment a million men and women, the *vignerons* of the globe, tend and guard the vines. They are raking and weeding between the ranks; they are pruning and the clip of *sécateurs* is like the sound of crickets; they are spraying, the 'first' spraying and the 'second' spraying, and overnight the vines are copper-blue as though lakes lay on the hillsides; they are staking and tying up the vines. Suddenly at the end of summer the figures are motionless. There is no one working in the vineyards. Only the swelling grapes move, and innumerable gravid bunches shift uneasily to hang freer from the leaves. Only the vines now work, preparing pleasure.

There are more than vineyards for comfort. I recall in sad moments the Dauphiné peasants scrambling with sacks to collect Génépi beside the very snouts of glaciers; the brakes of wild raspberry ripening in Tyrolese valleys for their consummation in Himbeergeist; the damsons and peaches that at Chantemesle were turned to good account; the rough apple trees of Calvados; the tufted palms, in whose tops the Egyptians, like ungainly birds, clamber to gather dates for Bouza; and the humble aniseed, growing that it may cloud my glass, even now preparing cloud-capped towers and palaces. The very fields belong to Dionysus: his are the harrowing and sowing, the first film of green, the ear and the bristling beard, barley growing on the downs, on the poorer land, among scarecrows and rooks under uncertain skies. All for pleasure, for straw-coloured bounty: Islay, Glen Mhor, Glenlivet, names that dispel accidie.

Sitting over the *gros rouge* Chez Jean, I found the valley too close for my divided mood. With a sense of betraying its trust, I escaped often to Paris, to more voices and more gestures. Yet Chantemesle followed me. Late at night I would seem to hear through the beat of drums and the ringing glasses the opening bars of the dawn-chorus, and I sometimes found through a haze of smoke the rootless dancers turning into trees. Leaving impulsively, I would search the night sky from the gutter's edge or drive hurriedly from the Grand Ecart to watch a late-rising moon from the heights above St Cloud. The birds, that no one now observed, saw in the first light my bleary-eyed returns to Chantemesle. As Michèle perhaps had been unwilling to share me with the valley, so now the valley would not accept divided loyalty. I sometimes came home as to a foreign country.

One morning after such a return, a feeling of guilt took me up the hillside instead of to my bed. It seemed an act of piety, an attempt to make amends for desertion. One of the first autumn mists clung to the river, a low mist from which the summits of the tallest trees were free, catching the early sun. Above me the sun was also brushing the tops of the bluffs, but the lower hillside where I emerged through the orchard was still in shadow. A heavy dew had fallen in the night. I also noticed – it came as a reproach – that Battouflet had been at work. Following the trail he had blazed, I found him lying at the edge of a copse. He must have been knee-deep in brambles when he fell the day before, overwhelmed by the summer tide as he flailed the suckers. Even dead he clutched the grass. His stick lay beside him. As I turned him stiffly over, my hands were wet with the dew that had soaked his jacket. The look in his blank eyes was as I had always known it; only the nervous grimaces had ceased. The sun reached us as I crouched there.

We buried Battouflet next day not far from the hamlet, in the narrow cavelike chapel, half-hewn from the hillside chalk, where a tablet now commemorates my Protestant parents, confounding those who proclaim the intolerance of the Catholic Church. His death was a small episode in the long history of the *côte*, but it marked for me the end of an epoch. No one would now attempt to clear the paths; nor, I realised, should I much longer leave my wake as I passed through the clinging thickets. Time was drawing me, unwilling as Battouflet, from the hillside.

The same afternoon I pushed out the canoe for the last time that year. Stepping into it was like stepping on a person asleep. It started and struggled. The disturbance sent ripples clucking under the boards in the boathouse and threw lace-light on the rafters. As the canoe swam into the stream, the same light was on the undersides of the trees. It was the river of unbroken glass, the summer river that seemed to flow below the surface, barely sucking at the boughs which dipped the water. Along the sandspits it curled like a cat, and parted from the prows of the islands without a murmur. The ripple of the canoe was no more than a water-rat might have made. The familiar craft provoked no movement on the islands, not a flicker in the green eyelids that shielded them. The banks were invisible, for the lids closed tight on the waterline. The green said nothing, and the blue canoe passed by. Though the knock of my paddle against the gunwhale sounded clear as the tap of a woodpecker, the birds were silent. I alone guessed the woodwarblers busy in the topmost branches, the pauses and spaces where the sunlight fell between the island trees, and the insects labouring through six-inch jungles. I alone knew the timeless time which had once existed there.

The canoe drifted with its grey shadow beside it. Then the shadow had gone. Branches brushed my head as the boat drew into a secret channel by the Firmin island. I was behind the leaves, within the green. Still nothing took note. No bird moved, though on the mud there were the footprints of moorhens. It was a year since I had been in the channel. With no one to clear a passage, the rushes had multiplied; they scraped against the boat on either side. A tree had collapsed and leant into the arms of another across the water. The canoe barely squeezed below the trunk. On the floorboards at my feet there were leaves and a caterpillar; a scarf of bindweed clung to a thwart. The current flowed slower than in the past; another decade and there would be dry land, an island less.

The green trembled. Nosing through the boughs, the prow of the blue canoe was again in the sunlight, again cast a shadow. From the gloom I emerged into the width of the main stream. Dazzled by the light, I was exposed and isolated on the sheet of water. The women banging their washing boards could see me from the Moisson bank, and I could count, screwing my eyes against the sun, the fishermen and their staked boats. Raising their heads, they must have thought, 'Strange. The blue canoe has come out from the middle of an island.' A pennant fluttered from a distant launch. A whiteness bubbled at the bows, and the curl of the streaming wake for a moment hid a skiff, so that two girls seemed to sit laughing on the water. Rippling along the distant shore, the wake rocked the staked boats and the fishermen nodded like dolls. Round a bend, a string of black barges slipped out of sight and the chug of their diesel died. In ten minutes, or twenty, or in an hour, the rhythm would start again, at first faintly, no more than the pulse of the summer afternoon, but as familiar to the river as the blue canoe, the note of the Moisson clock or the sound of the fishermen calling from boat to boat.

I was surrounded by shining water. I was far out from the islands, a brushstroke, a blue curve, perhaps a reflection of the sky. Now I could see, not the roofs of our house for they were hidden by the island trees, but the steep *côte* above. From Vétheuil to La Roche it stretched like a scroll, the detail perfect but the effect as flat as an oriental painting. The folds and combes were not apparent, and the copses, like islands of another sort, floated on the chalky turf. Even the bluffs gleamed flat in the sun. It was a hillside without contour, and since Battouflet and I were absent it was still.

On the other side were the Moisson spire and the houses gathered round it with their untidy orchards. Across the plain rose the coastline of the forest, dark because it lay in shadow with the sun behind. There birds preened in the abandoned aviaries, tree-ships sailed on the turf-swell and the pool at the quarry foot was like velvet. In the house where Clotilde now lived alone, the eggs in the cabinet were cradled in cotton-wool and the double folio on the lectern lay open at the *Festes à l'occasion du Mariage de Madame Louise-*

Elizabeth et Don Philippe. From the blue brushstroke on the water I could see the whole landscape – hillside, forest, islands – beautiful as it had ever been and apparently still as close; but mute. I was no longer part of it.

A week later I left with a sense of disloyalty and loss. Thirty years have not obliterated this sense, or the knowledge that I was most myself at Chantemesle. I have written this to make amends, a gesture of love.

About the Author

ROBIN FEDDEN (1908–77) was brought up largely in France, the son of water-colourist Romilly Fedden and his American wife, the novelist Katharine Waldo Douglas. Educated in France and England, he went to Cambridge to read English, though his outlook was deeply influenced by his continental childhood.

He travelled widely in the Middle East, serving briefly as Cultural Attaché at the British Legation in Athens. He then took up a post as lecturer in English Literature at Cairo University where, with Lawrence Durrell and Bernard Spencer, he edited *Personal Landscape*, one of the few literary periodicals of interest to appear during the war. After the war he worked for the National Trust and served as Historic Buildings Secretary and then Deputy Director-General until his retirement in 1973.

His eclectic nature is reflected in the books he left behind, which range from a study of suicide, a book of poetry and a paeon to mountains and mountaineering, *The Enchanted Mountains*, to several books on the National Trust and the English country house. Those who read his books on skiing are unlikely to know of his work on the crusader castles of Syria and the Lebanon. In *The Enchanted Mountains* and *Chantemesle* he shows his crystalline, poetic prose at its height.

He had passionate admirers and life-long friends in a variety of disparate disciplines. Like the mountains he so adored, he had a craggy sculptured face, and a strong, wiry physique which allowed him to explore their remotest slopes with hair-raising aplomb. As well as sitting on the committees of ski clubs, he was an eclectic connoisseur of antiquities and a father to two daughters.

ELAND

61 Exmouth Market, London EC1R 4QL
Email: info@travelbooks.co.uk

Eland was started thirty years ago to revive great travel books that had fallen out of print. Although the list soon diversified into biography and fiction, all the books are chosen for their interest in spirit of place. One of our readers explained that for him reading an Eland is like listening to an experienced anthropologist at the bar – she's let her hair down and is telling all the stories that were just too good to go in to the textbook.

Eland books are for travellers, and for readers who are content to travel in their own minds. They open out our understanding of other cultures, interpret the unknown and reveal different environments, as well as celebrating the humour and occasional horrors of travel. We take immense trouble to select only the most readable books and therefore many readers collect the entire, hundred-volume series.

You will find a very brief description of some of our books on the following pages. Extracts from each and every one of them can be read on our website, at www.travelbooks.co.uk. If you would like a free copy of our catalogue you can request one via the website, email us or send a postcard.

ELAND

'One of the very best travel lists' WILLIAM DALRYMPLE

An Innocent Anthropologist
NIGEL BARLEY
*An honest, funny, affectionate and
compulsively irreverent account of fieldwork
in West Africa*

Jigsaw
SYBILLE BEDFORD
*An intensely remembered autobiographical
novel about an inter-war childhood*

A Visit to Don Otavio
SYBILLE BEDFORD
*The hell of travel and the Eden of arrival
in post-war Mexico*

Journey into the Mind's Eye
LESLEY BLANCH
*An obsessive love affair with Russia and
one particular Russian*

The Way of the World
NICOLAS BOUVIER
A 1950's roadtrip from Serbia to Afghanistan

The Devil Drives
FAWN BRODIE
*Biography of Sir Richard Burton,
explorer, linguist and pornographer*

Turkish Letters
OGIER DE BUSBECQ
*Eyewitness history at its best: Istanbul during
the reign of Suleyman the Magnificent*

Two Middle-Aged Ladies in Andalusia
PENELOPE CHETWODE
*An infectious, personal account
of a fascination with horses,
God and Spain*

My Early Life
WINSTON CHURCHILL
*From North West frontier to Boer War
by the age of twenty-fivet*

A Square of Sky
JANINA DAVID
*A Jewish childhood in the Warsaw
ghetto and hiding from the Nazis*

Chantemesle
ROBIN FEDDEN
*A lyrical evocation of childhood
in Normandy*

Viva Mexico!
CHARLES FLANDRAU
*Five years in turn-of-the-century
Mexico, described by an enchanted Yankee*

Travels with Myself and Another
MARTHA GELLHORN
*Five journeys from hell by a great
war correspondent*

The Weather in Africa
MARTHA GELLHORN
*Three novellas set amongst the
white settlers of East Africa*

The Last Leopard
DAVID GILMOUR
*The biography of Giuseppe di Lampedusa,
author of* The Leopard

Walled Gardens
ANNABEL GOFF
An Anglo-Irish childhood

Africa Dances
GEOFFREY GORER
*The magic of indigenous culture
and the banality of colonisation*

Cinema Eden
JUAN GOYTISOLO
*Essays from the Muslim
Mediterranean*

A State of Fear
ANDREW GRAHAM-YOOLL
*A journalist witnesses Argentina's
nightmare in the 1970s*

Warriors
GERALD HANLEY
Life and death among the Somalis

Morocco That Was
WALTER HARRIS
*All the cruelty, fascination and
humour of a pre-modern kingdom*

MY BEGINNER'S GUIDE TO
CRYPTOCURRENCY

CRYPTO
MADE
CLEAR

HOLLY-ELLEN STOCKLEY

Cover image by: Yesna99, 99 Designs
Book design by: SWATT Books Ltd

Printed in the United Kingdom
First Printing, 2021

ISBN: 978-1-8384925-0-2 (Paperback)
ISBN: 978-1-8384925-1-9 (eBook)

Holly-Ellen Stockley
Email: hello@cryptocountess.com
Website: www.cryptocountess.com
Instagram: @cryptocountess

Table of Contents

Preface

Financial advice notice: Before you begin reading this book, I need to clearly state that my opinions are not financial advice. I am not a financial advisor, nor am I trained within the financial world. All thoughts and opinions are my own and all evidence has been put forward through my own research. It is up to you to conduct independent research before making any decisions to invest your money within cryptocurrency.

Never invest more than you are willing to lose and do not risk money you require to live, e.g. do NOT play with your mortgage or rent money!

Now, enjoy the journey!

CHAPTER 1:

Introduction: The Author's Journey

This book began life as a collection of my thoughts, findings, research notes and general information, all gathered from my journey into the cryptocurrency world.

I entered this world on a whim, without any knowledge of it at all. I just decided, one day in December 2019, after reading a news article, that I would buy some Bitcoin. I was naïve, had done no research, had no idea what I was doing and didn't understand the market or industry at all. I literally googled 'where is the best place to buy Bitcoin', which brought up a list of websites I now know to be called 'exchanges'. One of these websites was 'Coinbase' – I'll be explaining exchanges in more detail in Chapter 6. I decided that it looked like an easy to use and well-designed site, so I downloaded it, linked it to my bank account and invested £50.00. Whilst this might seem reckless, looking back it was the best, most random thing I have ever done.

I did nothing further – I just watched the value of my investment go up and down. I remember telling a friend I had bought some Bitcoin and had made 10p. Her response was, "That's nice Holly", and then she changed the conversation. Even later, when I started doing well in my trades, my father told my Nana that I'd been "trading fake coins online". (Her reply was that she didn't know what that was but was proud of me anyway). Not a lot of people, I have found, especially in my circle of friends and family, know much if anything about the cryptocurrency world. Those that have heard of it think it's a scam and the rest aren't bothered. As I have progressed and learnt more my immediate family have been forced to listen to my findings, and my parents are now both involved in cryptocurrency as well.

Working as self-employed within the beauty and design industries since 2011, and as an Aesthetic Practitioner specialising in Semi-Permanent Make-Up since 2016, I was forced to look for alternative means of income when the UK went into a national lockdown in March 2020 due to the coronavirus pandemic. Government restrictions prevented me from working and there was uncertainty on when, and how, measures would be lifted.

So, I decided to take cryptocurrency seriously and learn how trading the crypto market worked. However, I have never been good at maths and hated the subject at school. If I was in the education system now, I'm sure that my teachers would diagnose me with dyscalculia, as my brain struggles to problem-solve and understand mathematical equations. Nevertheless, I set myself a task to learn it, to believe in myself and trust that I could do it.

The more I read and learnt about the subject the more I struggled to find books and articles that really explained and broke down the cryptocurrency world in simple terms for people who knew absolutely nothing about it. Everything I read expected you to know something about finance or some aspect of cryptocurrency or trading which, as a complete novice, I found confusing. So, I began googling and researching articles, absorbing as much information as I could and recording it for reference for when I started trading.

Over the second half of 2020 my trading in cryptocurrency enabled me to turn my life and bank balance around. Whilst not 'out of my financial tunnel' yet I see some light. I feel confident, with improved self-worth and self-love. My belief, that cryptocurrency will continue to change my financial situation for the better, has led me to want to write this book.

I hope it provides key information and guidance to understanding the cryptocurrency world, to help others starting from scratch who have no experience and potentially the same lack of confidence with maths and figures.

Cryptocurrency has already begun to integrate itself into our 21st century world. I hope this book helps to show that when rules and patterns are followed in trading, risks can be minimised, losses reduced, and most importantly – money made!

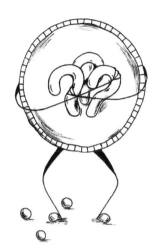

CHAPTER 2:

What is Cryptocurrency?

Cryptocurrency, or crypto for short, is a type of digital or virtual money. It has no physical counterpart such as a banknote or coin that can be carried around and it only exists in an electronic format.

Digital currency has been around for many years, it's just that we don't think about it that way. Your standard fiat funds, which is the currency of your country such as the Great British Pound (GBP) or United States Dollar (USD), are held in your bank account, which is then accessible from your online internet banking platform. For example, in the United Kingdom we have the Great British Pound. I have multiple bank accounts, as do many people, which hold funds for different things. If I want to move some GBP from one account to another bank account, I simply log onto my online banking and transfer it. It is something we don't even think about, as it is just part of our everyday life. But this is a form of digital currency.

Cryptocurrency, like digital fiat money, is a form of digital currency. I can send it and move it around online between different locations. I can pay in cryptocurrency on certain websites and I can also withdraw certain cryptocurrencies from designated crypto ATMs into GBP cash.

Cryptocurrency was initially created to address problems associated within our current financial and banking infrastructure with centralisation, security and confidentiality. Centralisation is the traditional method whereby there is a central supervisory authority responsible for decisions made within that organisation. This level of control and authority has led to multiple issues with asset management and control, which is a key part of why cryptocurrency was created. Cryptocurrency has many different uses and every crypto asset that has been, and is being created at present, tackles a different problem. They each have their own technologies and goals, covering a wide range of things such as online banking, faster payment processing, mortgages, loans, gaming, musician and artist royalties. You name a problem and there is probably a crypto asset out there being developed to solve it.

When people talk about cryptocurrency, they tend to talk or think about Bitcoin. This then leads people to either zone out of the conversation or say, "Oh I've heard of that, isn't it a scam?" The great thing though about the general public having an enormous misconception about the digital currency market is that it leaves more of an untapped market for the keen ones who are eager to understand and learn more about things they don't know. To fail to understand something just because it is new or scary is where so many people falter in life. They stick to their normal, what they know and what their circle of friends and family knows. By sticking to what society deems to be normal is how we function as human beings. We do what everyone else is doing – that is life. But it doesn't have to be. You don't have to believe what everyone else does. You don't have to work a 9-5 job just because that is what most people do. We live in an era of such great possibilities and opportunities. Failure to take advantage of these and accept how our lives and social structures are changing, is simply foolish.

We can be better. We can do better. You are better than the person you were yesterday just by wanting and thinking about changing elements of your life. It is so important that we grow as a human race, but unfortunately history tells us that this is what also holds us back. Our fear of movement, of change, of an alteration to the normality we are used to, is what keeps us in those dead-end jobs. It prevents us from rocking the boat and trying out new things, but this is where crypto can slide into your life on a gradual basis, changing it slowly and gently so that you don't even realise how much you are rocking the boat because it becomes your new normal. Before you know it, you are earning more through trading than you are working your 9-5. You are then in a position to quit your job and start living in a new way. A better, more positive way, with your time being better spent and your quality of life improving ten-fold.

Amongst all the negativity that Covid-19 has brought to the world, it has highlighted how quickly our normal life can be disrupted and how we need to adapt and change in order to move forward. Many people are now working in ways they haven't before due to this virus, and some positive things need to be taken from this change in habits. I do not believe that it is a coincidence that we have seen such an increase in the demand for cryptocurrency since Covid-19 and more people being at home and wanting to learn and earn differently.

Cryptocurrency, whether you want to believe it or not, (and hopefully you do which is why you are reading this book), is here to stay and I truly believe it will help change the world for the better.

When people question the longevity and durability of cryptocurrency and how it can be integrated within our world, it is critical to look at institutions like Forbes who now have a dedicated section in their online *Money* news category for articles about cryptocurrency. Why would such financially respected and long-standing organisations take the time to dedicate sections of their website to something that was a passing fad?

As much as some people like to think that the likes of Bitcoin are part of a fraudulent Ponzi scheme, I don't believe it is, and the evolution of digital currency is only going to get bigger and integrate further into our society and infrastructure. Now, this being said, cryptocurrency can be manipulated quite easily by traders referred to as whales. These are traders who hold large amounts of cryptocurrency and can move the market up or down depending on their desired outcome. This market manipulation can be horrendous and is responsible for the enormous up-and-down movements the market can see in one day, but these same moves are what make it exciting and, most importantly, make you money!

The cryptocurrency market, just like every currency market, is also affected by the stock market and worldwide events. A key example of this is a phenomenal crash crypto experienced in March 2020 when coronavirus began causing entire country lockdowns around the world, shutting down economies and releasing fear and uncertainty into the markets. This crash saw Bitcoin move from above $10,000 to $3,500. As you can imagine this kind of crash caught a lot of people off guard and caused a lot of people to get liquidated and lose all their money. One thing to bear in mind with any kind of cryptocurrency is that it is volatile. The market can experience these massive moves with no warning, and it is then that preparing in advance for a split-second crash could save your entire trading balance. We will talk later about how to protect your trading wallet and limit the worry of these things happening.

This book has been designed to not only introduce and explain the cryptocurrency world, but to also put forward the initial steps for learning how to trade crypto too. Learning how to understand and read a chart is an important element of trading successfully, but mindset plays a key part too and is something we will go into further detail later on. Without the right mindset from the beginning, you simply can't learn to trade and trade successfully! I never thought I would be

A Whale: A whale is someone who holds a lot of cryptocurrency. They hold large amounts of digital currency and can cause carnage with their trading due to the enormity of their wealth. They are able to rock the market through their trades which is why it is important to pay attention to certain whales and their trades.

successful in trading cryptocurrency due to my hatred of maths and of trying to understand graphs and charts. But I believed I could and would understand how to do it and now I can analyse and read charts without my brain hurting.

Choosing to venture into the world of cryptocurrency is something that I personally believe will be one of the best decisions you will ever make. By learning to trade online, you can literally work anywhere in the world, providing of course you can get an internet connection. It really does open up your options. Once you learn how to successfully trade repeatedly, you can quit a job you hate, you can travel the world, you can go to your child's school play, because your work now works around you!

All these things are what keep me pushing and striving to learn and be better. When I have bad trading days and the market is just going against all the indicators I follow and switches on me, I do sit there and think, why am I doing this?! I could just go and get an easy job with little stress, but then I remember I need to be my own boss. I want that freedom to work when I want to, to be able to spend what I want to and not worry about whether I can cover my card bill at the end of the month. I want to wake up and be happy and excited for my day, to spend more quality time with my family and friends. I want a better life. So, I keep going and suck up the bad days and put all that energy into being better and trading better.

You must use your losses as learning experiences, otherwise they will pull you down and prevent you from being successful.

With trading you can spend as much or as little time on it as you want to, depending on what kind of trader you want to become. In a few chapters' time, we will break down the different types of trader there are. The good thing is that, depending on what kind of trading day it is, you can change what type of trader you are that particular day! Cryptocurrency offers flexibility. It is a market that is open 24 hours a day, 365 days a year and which, I believe, offers unlimited earning possibilities.

At the back of this book in Chapter 15 you will find a useful glossary where we cover the basic and most common terminology, phrases and words you will come across as you enter the cryptocurrency and trading world. This is not a complete glossary of all things crypto, but I have tried to include many of the most common phrases and terminology I have encountered to date. As this book progresses, whilst I will try to explain each new crypto word or phrase as I use it, please refer to Chapter 15 for a more in-depth description as hopefully the word or phrase will be there!

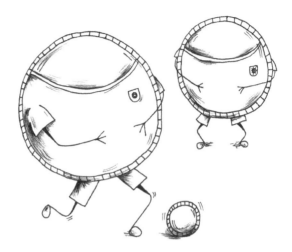

CHAPTER 3:

The Key Players

As at January 2021, there are approximately 5,760 cryptocurrencies being traded, with a total market capitalisation or value of $237 billion. Sadly, most of these cryptocurrencies will never achieve any kind of real tradable market volume and will just disappear off into internet space.

Despite there currently being so many cryptocurrencies within the market, there are just a few key players that you really want to own or have a piece of, investment-wise. Alongside the main currencies we will talk about in a moment, there are a few smaller alt coins that have gained greater momentum over the past few months and have been earmarked as being worthy of long-term investment.

As we talk about each cryptocurrency, you will see some letters in brackets next to each coin. These are the symbols which represent each coin and are used within the trading market to abbreviate each cryptocurrency, just the same as the Great British Pound is abbreviated to GBP or the United States Dollar is USD.

Bitcoin (BTC & XBT)

First up we have Bitcoin. This is the big, main, king boss everyone knows about. If you've heard about crypto, you've heard about Bitcoin. Bitcoin was the first cryptocurrency and is a decentralised peer-to-peer network, meaning that no single institution or person controls it. A Bitcoin cannot be printed and only 21 million Bitcoins can ever be created or mined – we will discuss mining shortly.

Bitcoin was introduced in 2009 as an open-source software by an anonymous programmer, or group of programmers, under the alias Satoshi Nakamoto. Open-source software is a type of computer software that is released in such a way that it gives users the rights to use, study, change and distribute it to anyone for any purpose. To this day, no one knows the true identity of Nakamoto, although there is constant speculation over who could be Bitcoin's creator. Despite this anonymity, a gentleman called Gavin Andresen was known by the alias Nakamoto when he/they stepped back as a lead developer from the coin in 2010.

Andresen has since released statements following Nakamoto's move to further decentralise the coin. In April 2011, Forbes quoted Andresen saying, "Bitcoin is designed to bring us back to a decentralised currency of the people." He also claimed: "This is like better gold than gold". The main advantage of Bitcoin is its independence from governments, banks and corporations. No authority can interfere with Bitcoin transactions, impose transaction fees or seize the coin. Moreover, the entire trading movement of Bitcoin is transparent – every single transaction is stored in a distributed public ledger called a blockchain. As Bitcoin is not being controlled by any authoritative figure, this gives its users total control over their finances.

Blockchain is a computerised technology that records transactions between two parties, so think of a blockchain as the DNA of a digital currency.

One way I like to explain what and how a Blockchain works is using this analogy:

Imagine you run a café, and at the end of every day you take all your receipts and put them in a box, called a block. The next day you do the same but you put that day's receipts in a new box. By the end of the week, you will have 7 different boxes or blocks, which when put together form a nice neat box pile or blockchain. This blockchain contains every single transaction your café has had in a week. That is what a blockchain is an electronic version of.

It is a public ledger which contains every transaction ever processed, using encryption techniques to control and verify the transfer of funds. Most cryptocurrencies are built upon and use blockchain technology to record transactions, with Bitcoin being the first. Blockchain records every transaction made on that specific cryptocurrency's network, which in turn creates blocks. As cryptocurrency has no physical imprint, the blockchain allows it to be tracked in detail all over the web, so it cannot be copied or counterfeited.

If someone tries to change just one letter or number in a block of transactions, this will affect all the following blocks in the chain. Due to the blockchain being a public ledger, any mistake or fraud attempt can be easily spotted and corrected by anyone. Users' trading wallets can then verify the validity of each transaction. The authenticity of each transaction is protected by digital signatures corresponding to the sending addresses.

This is a level of transparency and traceability unimaginable in any conventional currency. Imagine being able to see details of every trade ever made on currency exchanges in the US dollar. With crypto, this has created a detailed audit trail of every transaction ever, providing the ultimate safeguard from fraud and scams, and yet also guaranteeing a level of anonymity to the trader, as we will explain below. The creators of crypto realised from the outset that this level of traceability was required for a currency which you cannot ever hold in your hand.

We will discuss the process of purchasing Bitcoin and other cryptocurrency in more depth in a few chapters time. However, to further explain how Bitcoin works there are a few things to be aware of now. Just like when you move your fiat currency from one online bank account to another, moving or "sending" cryptocurrency from one location to another follows a similar system, except these movements are all recorded on a blockchain. The verification process depends on the location in which you are sending your crypto, but with Bitcoin, usually it will take just a few minutes for a Bitcoin transaction to be completed. The Bitcoin protocol is designed so that each block takes about 10 minutes to mine.

Now, you might be having an information overload right now, which is totally normal. It took me a little while to read, read and re-read again to fully understand the concept. I have also just introduced another new phrase: 'to mine' which I also need to explain. Cryptocurrency mining, or crypto mining, is a process in which transactions for various forms of cryptocurrency are verified and added to the blockchain. This process is conducted by people who are known as crypto miners. Just as cryptocurrency is virtual, so is the mine in which they are working! Each time a cryptocurrency transaction is made, a crypto miner is responsible for ensuring the authenticity of information and updating the blockchain with the transaction.

Miners are employed by cryptocurrencies for their ability to conduct the incredibly complex process of verifying all transactions. They are essentially the cornerstone of many cryptocurrency networks, as they spend their time and their harnessing of computing power to undertake hugely complex mathematical calculations. This is referred to as the proof of work (PoW) protocol. Through this process, miners are responsible for creating new coins or tokens, as they receive their reward in that coin or token for successfully completing a PoW task. Proof of work makes it extremely difficult to alter any aspect of the blockchain, since such an alteration would require re-mining all subsequent blocks.

As I have mentioned before, only 21 million Bitcoins can ever be mined. Once all 21 million have been created by the miners, there will be no more. The current timeline for when the last Bitcoin will be mined is around the year 2140, so we have some time yet to accumulate enough personal supply!

Core reasons people are drawn to Bitcoin

Decentralisation: One of Nakamoto's main objectives when creating Bitcoin was for it to gain independence from any governing body or authority. It is designed so that every person and business, as well as every machine involved in mining and transaction verification, becomes part of a vast network.

Anonymity: Bitcoin offers a level of anonymity that is hard to come by in today's world. Your Bitcoin wallet does not need to personally link or identify you and therefore cannot be tracked or traced by any kind of authority, unlike a normal fiat bank account.

Transparency: The anonymity of Bitcoin is only relative, as every single Bitcoin transaction that ever happens, as we explained above, is stored in the blockchain. In theory, if your wallet address was publicly used, anyone can tell how much money is in it by carefully studying the blockchain ledger. However, tracing a particular Bitcoin address to a person is still virtually impossible.

Speed: The Bitcoin network processes payments almost instantaneously; it normally takes just a few minutes for someone on the other side of the world to receive payment. However, you can alter how much you wish to pay to send a transaction. The higher the fee you pay the quicker it is processed, although even with the minimum transaction fee it usually only takes around 10-20 minutes to process.

Bitcoin has two abbreviations within the trading market and these are BTC and XBT. BTC is the original and XBT is the new abbreviation given by the International Standards Organisation, as Bitcoin is now on their list as an internationally recognised currency. Their standards dictate that if a currency is not associated with a particular country then it should begin with an X, hence XBT.

In February 2021, Bitcoin hit the mainstream media again when Elon Musk, the man behind Tesla, came forward with the news that Tesla had purchased £1.1 billion of Bitcoin. He also stated that the company hoped to start accepting Bitcoin as a form of payment in the near future. This type of acceptance into mainstream society only further supports Bitcoin's positive future.

Other key players beyond Bitcoin

Ethereum (ETH)

Ethereum is often referred to as Bitcoin's little brother. After Bitcoin, it is the second most popular cryptocurrency held, and it is also a decentralised system. Like Bitcoin, this means it is fully autonomous and is not controlled by anyone. Ethereum is an altcoin, which is the word we use to describe all cryptocurrencies other than Bitcoin.

When comparing it to Bitcoin, it is important to recognise that these are completely different projects with entirely different goals and aspirations. As discussed previously, Bitcoin was the first ever cryptocurrency and money transfer system, built and distributed by a public ledger called a blockchain. Ethereum took this technology and expanded its capabilities, creating its own whole network with its own internet browser, coding language and payment system. Ethereum also enables users to create decentralised applications on its own blockchain. These applications can be completely new ideas or decentralised reworkings of already existing ideas.

The Ethereum system is supported by a global network of people known as 'nodes.' Nodes are volunteers who download the entire Ethereum blockchain to their desktop computers and enforce all the rules of ETH's system. This safeguard ensures that the network is honest, and for this oversight service, nodes receive rewards in return.

Ethereum's rules, along with other aspects of the network, are dictated by something called smart contracts. A smart contract is a self-executing contract between a buyer and a seller whereby the terms of agreement are written into lines of code. The code, and the agreed contents within it, exist across a distributed, decentralised blockchain network. Despite smart contracts having been first implemented elsewhere as early as 2009, these smart contracts are one of the most prominent and hyped features of Ethereum's platform.

The idea behind Ethereum was first released in 2013 by Vitalik Buterin and was then publicly announced in January 2014 by Buterin and a core group of other creators. The Ethereum platform provides its own cryptocurrency token called Ether. This was used in a crowd sale in 2014 to fund the further development of the platform. Technically, Ethereum is a software platform that aims to act as a decentralised internet as well as a decentralised application store. The system needs a currency to pay for the computer resources required to run an application or a program, which is where Ether comes in. This means Ether acts as a fuel for the decentralised app within the network as opposed to only operating as a digital currency.

Now, as we said before, Ethereum used a lot of Bitcoin's technology and then expanded on it. One of the biggest differences between Bitcoin and Ethereum is the supply available. Whilst Bitcoin has a hard cap of 21 million, the potential supply for Ether is practically endless. Ethereum also confirms transactions quicker on the blockchain than Bitcoin and has applications beyond just money systems that can be supported.

Ethereum allows developers to build and deploy decentralised applications, which means the potential for the Ethereum platform's apps are only limited by the creator's own imagination and creativity. The platform therefore has the potential to completely change how our society operates. For example, if you were buying a house, this transaction requires multiple services that charge commission and escrow fees. Ethereum's blockchain can enable its customers to trace the origin of the product they're buying whilst implementing smart contracts, ensuring the transaction is safe, fast and without any middleman needing to be involved.

One of the most exciting things about Ethereum, which is securing it as one of the most investable assets within the cryptocurrency world, is its integration into our economy via large, well-known businesses like Amazon and Microsoft. These two companies have built their new software platforms on Ethereum's blockchain, and their integration of this emerging technology can only encourage confidence in it.

Litecoin (LTC)

At the time of writing, Litecoin is currently the third most held cryptocurrency on Coinbase, after Bitcoin and Ethereum. The technology behind Litecoin is based on providing a faster payment system from one currency to another. Unlike Paypal or your traditional fiat banking, Litecoin processes and conducts its transactions in units of Litecoin. Like Bitcoin, Litecoin is decentralised and has been developed to improve on Bitcoin's shortcomings. It has earned industry support over the past few years and has a high trade volume and liquidity by using a faster block generation rate and the use of Scrypt, (yes spelt like that, see glossary) as a proof of work scheme. Scrypt is an algorithm which is computationally harder to mine, as it requires large amounts of memory power. By creating a harder proof of work scheme, Litecoin believed that their miners were better and more experienced, as it was harder and took them more time to verify every block.

Launched in 2011, Litecoin was created by a former Google engineer called Charlie Lee. Like Bitcoin, Litecoin is mined and is limited in how many can ever be circulated. Litecoin can be mined every 2.5 minutes as opposed to 10 minutes for Bitcoin – however, there will ultimately only ever be 84 million Litecoin in circulation. Currently the incentive to mine a Litecoin sees a miner receive 50 Litecoin for every successfully mined block. The block is then verified by mining software and made visible to any miner. Once verified, the next block enters the Litecoin blockchain. In October 2015, Litecoin halved the number of Litecoin awarded to each miner and, like Bitcoin, these halvings will continue until the 84th million Litecoin has been mined. Halvings do not happen in every cryptocurrency project. However, they represent an event in which the rewards miners receive for verifying transactions are halved. The purpose of this is to reduce the number of new coins being created by that specific network, and based on previous history, after each halving there is a dramatic increase in that cryptocurrency's value.

Current advantages of Litecoin compared to other payment system cryptocurrencies are its speed and its ability to handle more transactions, as it has a shorter block generation time.

As we mentioned before, when you move or send a cryptocurrency from one place to another, more often than not you will incur a transaction fee. This fee covers the fact a minor has to process and verify your transaction. Sometimes the companies you use to purchase or move that crypto will also charge a fee on top of the transactional fee, but one of the core competitive angles for new cryptocurrencies is to be the cheapest and quickest coin. Bitcoin can have high transactional fees, especially when the market is overloaded, so it can cost a lot more to move your money. The highest Bitcoin transaction fee has been $60. However, at the time of writing in February 2021, the average Bitcoin transaction fee is around $25.

Ethereum's transactional fee is currently around $20, so both these top cryptos have what is considered to be high fees. This is where coins like Litecoin stand out as their current average transaction fee is around $0.19. Whilst fees can be considered high on some coins, the benefits of extensive verification and decentralisation outweigh this negative.

Some traders don't think much of Litecoin – however, its technology is something not to be dismissed and it has the potential to make huge gains in the future.

Ripple (XRP)

Next in our cryptocurrency line-up is Ripple which, at the time of writing, is having a bit of a rough ride. Ripple is both a platform and a currency that also allows everyone to use it to create their own currency via their own network called RippleNet.

RippleNet is a network of institutional payment providers such as banks and money services, that use solutions developed by Ripple to provide a problem-free, easy experience when sending money globally. XRP is the abbreviation for Ripple and is the token used for representing the transfer of value across the Ripple network. The main purpose of XRP is to be the mediator for other exchanges, including both fiat and cryptocurrency. For example, if you needed to exchange pounds into euros, Ripple can be both the pound and the euro, to minimise commission charges, with extremely low transaction costs of just $0.00001.

Originally created as a working prototype in 2004, it wasn't until 2013 when the creator of another network called Jed McCaleb managed to gather a few angel investors together to invest in Ripple Labs.

Unlike both Bitcoin and Ethereum, Ripple doesn't have a blockchain and instead has its own patented technology called the Ripple protocol consensus algorithm (RPCA) to verify transactions. The idea behind using a consensus platform is that every node must agree with the rest for the transaction to process. If one doesn't, then nothing will happen until their problem is rectified and a consensus reached.

Ripple was originally designed as a day-to-day payment system with quicker and cheaper transactions than Bitcoin. Its main focus is for it to be implemented within the mainstream banking network and therefore it has started an official organisation in order to be recognised. It currently supports the likes of Santander and Union Credit. The level of trust it has acquired by forming itself as an official organisation means that the more banks that use it as their transaction platform, the better the return on investment for Ripple investors. It boasts a low commission currency exchange, and the ability to process international transactions in around 4 seconds.

However, one of the main drawbacks for Ripple investors is the fact that it is highly centralised. The whole idea of cryptocurrency is to avoid centralisation control but, as Ripple tokens are already mined, the developers can decide when and how much to release or not to release. This means that investing in Ripple is like investing in a bank, and this can be controlled by Ripple Labs as they own 61% of the coins.

In December 2020, Ripple experienced a major setback which has consequently led to it being de-listed from many exchanges for US customers. This setback took the form of the Securities and Exchange Commission filing a lawsuit against Ripple Labs Inc and two of its executives. The lawsuit alleges that they have raised over $1.3 billion through an unregistered, ongoing digital asset securities offering. In layman terms, this means that the SEC think Ripple has falsely represented itself as a currency instead of as a security, similar to a stock or share. This uncertainty led to a tremendous sell-off, seeing the cryptocurrency plummet over 70%. However, there are still buyers picking up cheaper price points, so it isn't dead in the water just yet. The outcome of this case will determine how society and buyers view the company, and ultimately will decide its fate. Many people still think Ripple is a strong investment due to its integration possibilities within mainstream banking, but only the next few years, whilst their platform is tested and the lawsuit resolved, will show whether Ripple will be the long-term asset within society that it would like to be.

Cardano (ADA)

Cardano is currently one of the most talked about cryptocurrencies on the market and is a project set for big things in the next few years! Between Jan and Feb 2021 this cryptocurrency rose 311%! It is the world's first peer-reviewed blockchain and the platform maintains the operations of the ADA cryptocurrency. This platform allows for the fast movement of money, which is guaranteed to be secure through their technology. It is a third-generation cryptocurrency and smart contract platform that is designed to improve scaling problems that both Bitcoin and Ethereum have struggled with. It was originally conceived in 2015 by Charles Hoskinson, who also happens to be one of the co-founders of Ethereum, so Cardano is an evolution of the Ethereum technology.

The Cardano platform and blockchain is made up of two layers. The Cardano Settlement Layer (CSL) and the Cardano Computation Layer (CCL). The CSL is used to settle transactions that use ADA, such as transferring ADA between accounts and recording transactions. The CCL contains the smart contract logic that developers can leverage to programmatically move funds. Designed to be integrated within the mainstream financial ecosystem, the heart of Cardano's platform is Ouroboros, which is an algorithm that uses proof of stake protocol to mine coins. The proof of stake (PoS) protocol was created as an alternative to the proof of work protocol (PoW) to tackle issues with the latter. The proof of stake concept means that a person can mine or verify block transactions according to how many coins they hold. This means that the more they own of that coin, the more mining power they have.

Unlike proof of work which uses a lot of energy to answer and solve puzzles, a proof of stake miner is limited to mining a percentage of transactions that is reflective of their ownership stake. For instance, a miner who owns 5% of the coin available can theoretically only mine 5% of the blocks.

Cardano believe this system will provide their network with a greater level of security and performance. Their layered design, with a settlement layer and computational layer, allow the system's capacity to grow as users join, getting larger with time.

In July 2020, Cardano introduced its Shelley Mainnet, a decentralized network of community nodes that operate on a proof of stake protocol, with less central governance from the developers. This next phase of the Cardano development has greatly boosted the cryptocurrency's stature within the community and, with a further three more upgrades intended to take place in the future, it is marked as a 'one to watch' currency, set to make large profits and returns for investors in years to come.

So, that is an outline of the distinctive features of Bitcoin and four other major cryptocurrencies. As at Jan 2021, there were in fact more than

4,000 cryptocurrencies in existence, with new ones being set up all the time. However, these five are, in my opinion, the key ones to look at, especially if you are new to crypto. At the beginning of this book there is a financial statement which I feel needs to re-iterated here. I am not a financial advisor and whilst the coins I have spoken about above have gained enormous traction in the crypto world, there are many more poised to run at any moment. The wonderful thing about crypto is that you don't need to have a certain amount of money to invest and get started. You can buy certain cryptocurrencies for less than 1p! When Bitcoin was first released no one wanted to buy it and it began trading in 2010 at around $0.0008! Imagine how you would feel now if you bought back then. Any new crypto project has the potential to be the next Bitcoin, so all you need to do is ensure that your research on whatever you choose to invest in is sound.

The DeFi Revolution

Following on from the key players in the cryptocurrency world it is vital we now talk about something called DeFi. DeFi is the abbreviation for Decentralized Finance and is an ecosystem of financial applications built upon blockchain networks like Ethereum. DeFi represents a movement that is focused upon creating financial services that are transparent and permission-free. This means that financial products can be created which are accessible internationally by everyone and can operate, unlike a bank, without a central authority.

As of November 2020, there were 215 DeFi projects listed and 203 of them are built on Ethereum. These projects are software protocols that are being developed to run off a blockchain network in order to automate financial services. The main difference between DeFi projects and cryptocurrencies is the fact that DeFi focuses on decentralization while offering lucrative incentive structures to encourage investors to take part in the movement.

DeFi projects aim to solve issues within our historic financial service industry such as those affecting lending, investment, wealth management and insurance. Let's take moving money from one country to another as an example. Currently, if you were to send money abroad it would more than likely take around three working days to process through a third party and you could pay anywhere up to 10% in fees. However, a certain type of DeFi cryptocurrency could carry out this transaction in minutes, without the involvement of a bank account or third party, at a much lower cost, whilst you remained in control of the underlying asset.

Changes like this, such as increased speed and improved access to funds, are set to reinvigorate the process by which we lend, borrow and exchange money, and earn interest. I have been a bit slow to really invest in the DeFi party if I'm honest. I was so involved with learning about all the main cryptocurrencies that, despite seeing my newsfeed and the forums start to talk about these projects, I didn't pay much attention to it.

One DeFi project that caught my eye due to its gigantic moves was Yearn Finance (YFI). Its value moved up $10,000 in a day without breaking a sweat! The more I looked into these DeFi projects, the more I realised this was a movement which could help to do nothing less than shape the future of our entire financial system. As a result, I became more interested in following and trading them.

DeFi projects are another example of how the cryptocurrency industry is continuously evolving to change and revolutionise the way we use and interact with money. The innovation that DeFi projects offer may seem unsettling to the traditional financial markets for many reasons. Some DeFi projects offer customers higher returns on their investment than a traditional bank whilst others open up the possibility for consumers who wouldn't normally qualify for loans or even mortgages to use their cryptocurrency as a deposit. There are currently projects in the making to allow people to borrow against their Bitcoin. This would open up the possibility of home ownership to a massive new market of people that mainstream banks would sniff at. The potential to use technology and blockchains to further eliminate the need for third party involvement, in this case the need to secure a mortgage from a mainstream bank, is exciting and thrilling and opens up so many opportunities for us as consumers.

The top DeFi projects I currently follow are:

- Chainlink (LINK)
- Uniswap (UNI)
- Aave (AAVE)
- Dai (DAI)
- Maker (MKR)
- Compound (COMP)
- Yearn.Finance (YFI)
- SushiSwap (SUSHI)
- 0x (ZRX)

As with any kind of information, it is so important for you to conduct your own independent research. I am not recommending that you invest in any one specific cryptocurrency or project, and there are so many more excellent opportunities that I have not even mentioned here! Part of what makes crypto so exciting is the pace at which it is evolving and developing, and inevitably, the information in this book is just a snapshot in time, based on the current information I had at the time of writing. Please undertake your own due diligence on every project and crypto technology before you choose to trade or invest in it.

CHAPTER 4:

The Essential Starter Kit

Before we discuss the initial steps to get into the trading element of cryptocurrency, we need to look at the basic things that you will require before you even think about learning how to trade. These may seem over-simplified – however, this book is designed to take a complete novice from knowing nothing to being able to understand what is needed to trade cryptocurrency.

The main things you will need are:

» **A secure internet connection:** This should be a secure private connection. Public wi-fi platforms are often sketchy and can allow anyone to monitor what you are doing, leaving you wide open to hacks. Something we do not want when trading! The best option for private trading is to open each trading platform in a private window. This can be selected as an option when you open a new internet browsing tab. The other option is to trade via a virtual private network (VPN). This is a protective barrier in the sense that it hides your internet location and prevents hackers from seeing your browsing location. VPNs vary in price, but it is now quick and easy to set one up and, in my opinion, it is an essential investment, especially when you start trading large amounts.

» **A secure device:** Next you will need a device that allows you to access the internet. I find a laptop or desktop easier than my phone or tablet just because I can see more on my screen and control my trades far better. Again, once you are trading large amounts it is advisable to increase the safeguards you put in place. Ideally, invest in a dedicated, separate device, such as a laptop that you now only use for the purpose of crypto trading. In this way you will prevent your browsing history from picking up damaging content and thus leading to hacks.

» **Access to note-taking:** I always have a notepad or a writing application such as Word, or Pages on a Mac, open on my laptop so that I can make notes or jot down ideas and opinions on how I feel the market is moving on any specific day, and how I can take advantage of this.

» **A trading spreadsheet:** I prefer to use Excel, but you can also use Numbers on Mac. This is to track what you do and be accountable for your mistakes because, trust me, you will make them! Being able to track every trade you make not only helps you to see your progress, but also helps you to see where you went wrong on a trade and learn from that moving forward. Having a bad trade is inevitable – it happens to everyone no matter how long you have been trading but knowing why a trade went against you is key to ensure you don't pick up bad habits. By keeping track, you can see if you are using too high a leverage or risking too many contracts on a trade. I'll explain these trading concepts shortly.

» **A relaxed environment to work:** This seems so simple but is so, so important! Trading is stressful and when learning how this all works, you need to be focused and relaxed. Chaotic environments or loud places are not going to help you concentrate. You need to have no distractions, in a space that is clutter free and helps to relax your mind.

» **Be calm:** This is even more important than finding a relaxed environment. Never enter into trading when you are drunk, tired, frustrated or restless! Again, this may seem obvious but if your mind isn't focused and in tip-top condition, your trades will be all over the place and that is when you will lose money!

So, these are the main things you need to have ready before we go any further.

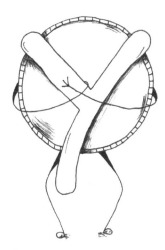

CHAPTER 5:

Trading Crypto – Identify Your Why

Before we dive deeper into the aspects of trading cryptocurrency, I want to first explain a little more about why I got into this world and why I chose to learn how to trade cryptocurrency. This may prompt some nods of recognition and help you to identify your own *Why* for trading crypto. It's so important that you work through those thoughts, as your *Why* will help you to set your priorities, your limits and your goals for your crypto trading.

Every new year I set myself a goal and this normally takes the form of wanting to learn a new skill or take a new course to improve my income in relation to my aesthetics business. Ever since I was little, I've believed that one day I would be truly successful and not have to worry about money again, and this belief has always pushed me to want to improve myself and do anything I can to earn more and be more productive.

In January 2019 I was writing down potential things I could expand on at work and realised I was already trained in everything I wanted to be. This led me to look outside of my general work environment and question what other new things I wanted to learn. As I have mentioned in my introduction, maths and I have always had a tumultuous relationship – however, one thing I wrote down on my goal list was the possibility of learning and understanding the stock market.

I've worked for myself since I was 19 years old, and I have never liked being told I can't do something – yes you can imagine how much of a bratty child I was – I am still apologising to my mother about my childhood behaviour! But the point is, despite knowing that maths and that level of concentration and focus was not my forte, I wanted to at least try and see if I could learn about stocks. I did some research and bought 4 or 5 books that were recommended as the "top" ones to read to gain a basic concept of this subject. I started a few but honestly found them really dull and so quickly lost motivation and interest. Not wanting to be defeated by my own lack of desire to read more about the stock market I began researching other ways, ideas and avenues people use to invest and make money. As the year passed, I continued to work in aesthetics but still hadn't found anything that jumped out at me to make more money on the side, particularly as the stock market still bored me. It was first December 2019 when I started to see and read things about Bitcoin and finally here was something which intrigued me! I decided to just take a punt on it. Back then I didn't realise how those first naïve steps into crypto would change my life and self-belief so much!

My relationship with finances has never been a bad one and both my parents have always been avid investors in property and saving etc, but as I approached 30, I felt more and more pressure to be successful and reach those financial milestones that are so prevalent within our society. I had accumulated debt from my bachelor's and master's degrees, as well as my investment into training in the aesthetics world, which is not a cheap industry to work in. I felt like I was constantly working to just pay off credit cards and never really managed to save anything. Maybe all this sounds familiar! If you are in your 20s, 30s or maybe even older, running hard just to stand still financially seems to be the way things are in the 21st century.

And then, wham, Covid-19 hit and, like most of us, this put my financial situation into even greater turmoil. I was forced to stop work and found myself burning through what few savings I had at a frightening rate. Confronted with all this I knew that I had to find new ways to earn an income.

It is at this point I decided to really commit to learning and understanding cryptocurrency because I knew that if I could master this skill and teach myself how to trade and invest in this world, then I could really change my life. This may sound corny, but I didn't really have any other choice. It was no one's fault that I couldn't work, but it would be my fault if I didn't use the lockdown time to focus and try to make money somehow. I had £1,000 in an emergency, do not touch under any circumstances, safety bank account, and I decided to put that into crypto. Now, one thing I do preach in this book and you will often see in the crypto trading world in general, is do not play or trade with money you cannot afford to lose. Despite my financial situation being pretty dire, the £1,000 I had in my emergency account was something I never included in my budgets and so I wasn't relying on it for anything else. The way my brain was working at the time was, you have £1,000 to lose but you could gain a million.

I knew that I needed to change my financial situation. I wanted to look at my bank account and instead of shuddering and thinking, urgh, how am I going to find that, I could smile and sleep comfortably at night. I wanted to enjoy a freedom that would allow me to travel and work on my laptop from anywhere I liked. I wanted to support my family, even pay off my parents' mortgage one day and never be in debt again. These may sound like dreamy desires, but I know that if I really commit to this, I can achieve these things, one way or another.

On top of all the obvious benefits of being financially stable and free from debt, I wanted to learn and understand this world so that I could regain my confidence after the terrible effects of the pandemic. I wanted to prove to myself that I could do something that no one would ever expect of me and that I wouldn't even necessarily expect of myself. Believing you can do something is, in my opinion, one of the hardest skills you can master in life. It doesn't matter if you have the brain of Albert Einstein, if you don't believe in yourself and you don't have any self-worth, then what good is that wonderful brain to anyone?

I can only assume that you are reading this book because you want to learn more about cryptocurrency and trading, and maybe you are also seeking the same financial freedoms that I am. Whatever your *Why*, it is important to always have the bigger picture in your mind and know what you are working for. Ask yourself what you want to achieve. What are your financial goals? Why does cryptocurrency interest you?

For me, I see the cryptocurrency world as the fun little brother to the stock market. It is a world built upon freedom, new technologies and ideas, decentralisation and almost, pardon my French, sticking it to the big man of constitutional banking. As I mentioned in Chapter 3, cryptocurrency offers opportunities and opens a financial sector up to people that would never normally "fit" into our financial industries tick box. Imagine being able to finally qualify for a mortgage because you can borrow against your crypto. It is this excitement and innovation that really caught my eye as I researched this world more. As well as the ability to be a part of the foundation of so many cryptocurrencies and watching a portfolio grow in line with their growth, this made crypto a lot more interesting to me and made me want to earn money from it.

I know I'm not going to be a millionaire tomorrow, but I also know that I have managed to grow my initial £1,000 investment into a pot that has allowed me to not only keep my head above water with bills whilst being unable to work in my day job, but also start to chip away at my debt.

Your personal involvement with crypto can go as deep as you want it to. This may just be a little side hobby for you, or this might be something you want to turn into a full-time career. Much of how involved you want to become will depend on many factors such as: your current financial situation, your attitude to risk, how much time you have available to give to trading and also how long you want to hold that crypto asset. However deep you want to dive though, the opportunities and possibilities that this world can offer you are, in my opinion, endless.

By this point I hope you have started to answer some of your own questions about why you are reading this book and what you want out of crypto, so this now leads us nicely into looking in more detail at how we trade cryptocurrency.

Trading in cryptocurrency

By definition, trading in general is the activity of buying and selling. Now, with cryptocurrency, it is important to note that there are two ways you can trade, and I like to think of them as active trading and passive trading.

Active trading is what I would personally describe as the trading you do on a trading platform, where you are constantly buying and selling that crypto asset. This is something you would do every day or at least every week and is classed as short-term trading.

Passive trading is where you buy in at one price and then hold it, choosing to sell when it reaches your desired price point. Passive trading is something you may do every week or it could be something you only do every few years and therefore is considered long-term trading.

We will be looking at the crypto trading journey, which may seem daunting at the moment in that there is a great deal of information to process. However, when you break it down into small steps, it is easier to understand. To help with this too, throughout this chapter I will show you illustrative examples using a notional £100 investment in various trading situations. To summarise what we will be discussing in the following chapters, let's look at the basic steps you will take when starting to trade crypto:

1. Choose how much fiat currency you wish to start with, using my £100 example.
2. Choose an exchange you would like to use. An exchange is the place where you buy your crypto, open an account, send your fiat currency and then use this to buy your chosen crypto currency. This process is made simple by the exchanges and, don't worry, we will look at a few examples below. Many exchanges provide how-to videos or guides on their websites to give you step-by-step instructions on how to send or deposit your fiat currency to the exchange. We will cover the world of exchanges in the next chapter before tackling the process of trading in cryptocurrency.
3. Once your fiat currency is in the exchange you can then choose which cryptocurrencies you want to buy and how much of them!

Now, after step 3, this is where you might decide to stop trading and simply just buy and then sell your cryptocurrency at a higher price than you originally bought it. However, if you choose to progress further you can then:

4. Send your cryptocurrency to a trading platform and begin to actively trade it. We will get into the detail of trading in Chapter 7.

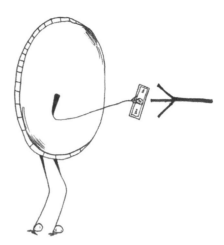

CHAPTER 6:

Using an Exchange

Before you can actively trade a crypto asset, you need to purchase cryptocurrency with your fiat money, for example the pound, euro or dollar.

Once you have decided how much of your fiat currency you wish to invest and trade with, in order to then buy cryptocurrency, you need to use an exchange. A cryptocurrency exchange, also known as a digital currency exchange (DCE), is a business that allows customers to trade cryptocurrencies or digital currencies for other assets, such as conventional fiat money or other digital currencies. Exchanges may accept credit card payments, wire transfers or other forms of payment in exchange for digital currencies or cryptocurrencies.

These exchanges vary in ability; some allow you to actively and passively trade, whereas others only allow you to actively trade.

An important thing to be aware of with all exchanges is their fees. These can vary and are often tricky to find. However, from my experience, the good news is that the initial depositing of your fiat currency from your bank account into an exchange to simply "sit" in their fiat wallet until you know what cryptocurrency you want to buy is free.

Some exchanges then offer introductory fees on purchasing cryptocurrency. For example, purchases within your first 30 days will be fee free, whilst other exchanges have a tiered fee system based on how much you are wanting to buy. Typically, exchange fees are 1-3%.

Coinbase is one of the largest and most well-known exchanges and this is the one I used when I first started trading. Another big player is called **Binance**, which also supports the purchase of many different cryptocurrencies. When I talk about 'support' here it means that they 'stock' that coin. Not all cryptocurrencies are available to purchase on every exchange – in fact some are only available on specific smaller exchanges. If there is a particular coin you are interested in purchasing, especially one that is less well known, it is important that you conduct thorough research on where you can buy it safely and securely, because there are smaller exchanges which can be scams.

Due to every country having different laws and regulations regarding online currency and cryptocurrency, not every exchange is supported and allowed to be accessed worldwide. As I am in the United Kingdom, these are some of the main exchanges that we can access and legally use, in no particular order:

- Coinbase
- Coinbase Pro
- Binance
- Crypto.com
- Kraken

As far as I am aware for the United States, Australia, Canada, New Zealand and the rest of the world, traders can also use Coinbase, Crypto.com, Kraken and Binance US; however, this does depend on which state traders live in. For example, regulation within the USA for cryptocurrency is currently changing and some exchanges are not supporting US customers from certain states at the moment. There are a few other exchanges that are popular with US customers – some examples of these are Phemex and Bittrex.

As the cryptocurrency market and its worldwide regulation is constantly evolving and changing, it is important to note that you must look at each exchange and consider if it suits your needs and is supported legally in your country. I also think it is important that you like the layout of that exchange and find it easy to use. You need to feel comfortable with its user interface and programming otherwise you will be overwhelmed with all the information on the platform.

Below are some pros and cons on the main exchanges that I have found. A common drawback with many of these exchanges, as you will see, is this: access to an exchange can go down for maintenance or not load when there are large market movements. This is due to the amount of people either trying to sell at high prices or buy in to big crashes. We will talk later on about safe places to store and hold your cryptocurrency, but these exchange issues reinforce why it is important to not store your crypto on exchanges long term.

Coinbase

Coinbase was launched in San Francisco in 2012 and is the largest cryptocurrency trading platform in the US. It is also ranked among the top crypto exchanges in the world by traffic, liquidity and trading volumes according to CoinMarketCap.com, a market research website.

Besides being a cryptocurrency brokerage, Coinbase also offers custodial services for cryptocurrency storage for institutions; a cryptocurrency payments platform for businesses; and its own cryptocurrency, USD Coin, a stable cryptocurrency linked to the US dollar.

Users are given the choice to trade on Coinbase or to upgrade to Coinbase Pro, which is a premium service that includes the ability to make crypto-to-crypto transactions and other advanced trading functions. Coinbase also provides a free online wallet for users on both iOS and Android platforms.

A wallet is where your cryptocurrency is stored. In Chapter 12 we talk in detail about how and where to store your cryptocurrency but to summarise for now, there are two places you can store your crypto: online and offline. An online cryptocurrency wallet is like the internet banking you would use for your fiat currency. Online wallets are places that store your crypto assets for you and take the form of exchanges, trading platforms and downloadable applications on your devices. For example, Coinbase offer the ability to hold your crypto on their online wallet. However, there is a saying within crypto of, "Not your keys, not your coins". This refers to the fact that if you do not have the "keys" which is what we refer to as passwords in crypto, then the cryptocurrency stored in online platforms could be hacked or stolen by a third party. The chances of you losing your crypto through an attack are slim and many exchanges are insured against hacks and exposure, but it is still not recommended to keep large sums online. It is therefore only advisable to keep your crypto on an online platform when actively trading and to regularly move profits off the exchange and onto your offline storage platform.

The best place to keep your crypto currency if you want to hold it for the long term is on something called a hard storage wallet or an offline wallet. This is also called a cold wallet because it is not connected to the internet all the time, only when you are transferring funds. Think of a hard wallet like your physical fiat wallet that holds your fiat notes. You have physical possession of it, unlike your online banking. An offline hard wallet is the safest place to keep your digital asset because no one can access it without a specific access code and series of passwords or "keys", which are created when you set up the hard wallet. A hard wallet allows you to hold the keys to your crypto as opposed to an online platform like Coinbase holding them. A hard wallet is a bit like a

USB stick in the sense you plug it into your device to access its content. As mentioned, we discuss the types of hard wallet available later.

It may seem strange to talk about hard storage wallets and offline wallets when cryptocurrency is an online, digital asset and has no physical counterpart. However, when we talk about online and offline storage, it just means the place you store it is either connected or not connected to the internet.

Another feature I really like about Coinbase is that you can 'stake' certain coins and earn money with them. Staking is when you place your crypto asset in a kind of 'pot' for a designated amount of time. You then earn interest, also called Annual Percentage Yield (APY), on the amount you have staked. This is a great way of making your crypto work for you and earn more of that particular asset.

For example: One cryptocurrency which Coinbase offer staking on is called Tezos. When you purchase Tezos with Coinbase you can opt in to stake them and their current APY is 4.63% per annum. So, if you purchased £100 worth of Tezos you would earn £4.63 interest if you staked it for one year. This is an excellent rate of interest – try securing anywhere close to that with your fiat currency!

Coinbase allows you to spot purchase cryptocurrency. This is where you buy at one price with no leverage and then sell when you want to – we talk about leverage later. You can use Coinbase to passively trade or just to purchase crypto before sending it to your desired trading platform.

For example: If I spot bought £100 worth of Bitcoin on Coinbase and then Bitcoin increased in price, my £100 could then be worth £150, at which point I could sell it if I wanted to.

Coinbase Pro allows you to actively trade with leverage, for example, I could use my £100 to buy £300 of Bitcoin. In order to do this, I need to trade with 3x leverage. However, I find the Pro platform a little intense and therefore it is not my preferred active trading platform.

Pros:

- Easy customer interface, friendly and easy to use the device app as well as website access
- Offers a wide range of cryptocurrencies
- Supports all payment methods for depositing fiat
- You don't need to deposit a large sum of money to start; less than £5/$5
- Coinbase has its own independent insurance for losses encountered due to theft or site hacks
- You can stake certain crypto assets

Cons:

- High transaction fees
- It can experience site outages when there are large market movements. Your money is always safe during these outages but it can be frustrating when you cannot access the site at critical trading times.
- Poor customer service

Binance

Binance was founded in 2017 by a gentleman called Changpeng Zhao and is now one of the world's leading cryptocurrency exchanges by trading volume. Zhao's goal for the exchange was to offer solutions to the numerous problems he saw within the cryptocurrency trading infrastructure. These included poor technical architecture, insecure platforms, poor market liquidity, poor customer support and poor language support.

Binance is an extremely popular exchange, as it offers multiple crypto assets and both a spot and margin trading option. However, in May 2019 it suffered some reputational damage when hackers stole over 7,000 Bitcoin from Binance, which at the time was equivalent to roughly $41 million. Zhao quickly took to social media to assure customers that their funds were safe and Binance used its own reserve to cover the costs of the stolen Bitcoin. Zhao tweeted **"Funds are #safu"** which meant that funds were safe. This has now become a commonly used crypto phrase in forums, and traders use it when they think their positions are solid.

Binance's licensee, Binance US, was established in late 2019 for American crypto traders, due to regulations brought in by the US. They required their own exchange which adhered to US law. In April 2020, the exchange made one of the splashiest acquisitions of the year when it bought CoinMarketCap, a cryptocurrency data provider, for a rumoured $400 million.

Pros:

— Has an easy-to-use interface and can be used by beginners and advanced users
— Offers both spot trading and margin/leverage trading
— Has multiple cryptocurrencies available
— Has a good device application as well as a desktop version
— Includes "how to read" visual representations for ease of learning to trade on their site
— Low trading fees
— Assets are insured in case of security breaches on the site. However, this does not cover personal security issues.
— Excellent customer service

Cons:

— Can suffer from site outages when there is a large market movement
— Does not support all payment methods for depositing fiat
— Currently Binance US does not support services in New York, Alaska, Alabama, Connecticut, Georgia, Hawaii, Florida, Louisiana, Idaho, North Carolina, Vermont, Washington and Texas due to missing regulatory requirements.

Kraken, Kraken Pro and Kraken Futures

Kraken was founded by Jesse Powell in 2011 and launched in 2013. It is a US-based cryptocurrency exchange and, according to CoinMarketCap, as of January 2021 it is the fourth largest crypto exchange in the world. One of the perks of Kraken is that it supports multiple US states and 176 countries worldwide, with over 40 cryptocurrencies available to purchase. It has three device applications. Kraken is the basic beginner's app which is where you can spot-buy assets. Kraken Pro allows you to leverage and is a more advanced system and Kraken Futures allows you to trade future contracts.

Pros:

- Supports more US states than most other exchanges
- User-friendly beginner platform
- Has ability to download a separate trading app for margin/ leverage trading called Kraken Pro
- Low transaction fees

Cons:

- The site can go down for maintenance quite often, especially during large market movements
- The interface, whilst simple in comparison to Binance, can take some getting used to in order to navigate what you are trying to do

Crypto.com

Crypto.com is a cryptocurrency, an exchange, an online wallet and a trading platform. Its main aim is to promote the widespread adoption of cryptocurrencies. It was founded in 2016 and already has over 3 million users. The company is headquartered in Hong Kong and is headed by seasoned entrepreneur Kris Marszalek. Crypto.com has its own token called CRO and, in another cool feature, they have partnered with Visa to create their own debit card. This enables you to use your cryptocurrency wallet on a day-to-day basis to spend on goods and services out in the world.

Crypto.com is the platform I am currently using for buying cryptocurrency due to their fees being slightly lower than Coinbase. It is just not practical in this book to list the fees charged by every exchange, as they change frequently and also depend on what cryptocurrency you are purchasing and how much of it you are purchasing. Some exchanges have tiered fees up to a certain investment amount and then, like with many other exchanges, you only know the exact fee an exchange is going to charge you for a transaction at the point when you commit to the purchase. When it shows you the applicable charges though it does give you the option to cancel the transaction if you think the fee is unreasonable. I have found from my experience that Crypto.com does tend to be lower than Coinbase though. As a ballpark range, as mentioned above, you will be looking at 1-3% for your exchange fee.

They also allow more coin staking options than Coinbase so you can earn more interest with them on flexible terms, which means you can take the crypto in and out of the staking pot, for up to three-month term periods, which is where you need to commit to keep the crypto staked for the full three-month period.

The longer you commit to keep your cryptocurrency in the stake pot, the higher the percent in APY or interest you will receive. However, these APY rates are subject to change at any time.

Pros:

- Easy to use app and online platform
- Quick transaction and deposits
- Multiple cryptocurrencies available to purchase

- Availability to stake multiple coins at high APY% rewards
- Has a Visa backed debit card with multiple rewards and card features

Cons:

- Transaction fees on buying cryptocurrency with fiat currency
- You can only access your account on the app from a device such as your phone or tablet. You can access the trading exchange from a desktop PC though.
- The app can go down for maintenance and not load when there are large market movements.
- Some cryptocurrencies require a minimum purchase in the app depending on their current value. There is also a minimum purchase requirement to stake certain cryptos.

So, that is a summary of just four of the major exchanges where you can buy cryptocurrency, and there are many others to choose from. As with other aspects of crypto, please conduct your own market research to find the perfect platform for you and your crypto needs.

Depositing and Withdrawing Crypto

Before we move on to talk about trading platforms, we need to explain how and why we move our cryptocurrency from the exchange. Having used your chosen exchange to buy some crypto – let's say, for example, you have bought some Bitcoin – we now need to move that Bitcoin into an account that will allow you to actively trade it, if this is what you would like to do.

Moving your money from one exchange to another, or from an exchange to a trading platform, is called withdrawing and depositing. You are withdrawing the amount and depositing it elsewhere.

When we send fiat currency online, we need to enter the sort code, account number and name of the person to receive that money. Sending crypto is similar to this, but instead of needing a sort code and account number you need something called an address. Every crypto account you have, whether it is on an exchange, a trading platform or a holding wallet, has its own individual wallet address. This address is also individual to that specific cryptocurrency, i.e. your Bitcoin has one address and your Ethereum has a different one. These addresses are often long and are made up of a mixture of numbers and letters. It is crucial that you never share your addresses with other people because they can use them to steal your crypto!

When you are sending crypto from one wallet to another, it can take anywhere from a few minutes to a few hours. This is where the blockchain comes into play and every transaction must be verified on it before the crypto is deposited in its new account. So, while these various processes can sound long-winded, they have been imposed each step of the way as security and verification checks to protect each transaction.

Sometimes you can increase the level of fees you wish to pay for this movement, for it to be verified quicker, although sometimes this option isn't available. It just depends which exchange or trading platform you are using.

One final thing to remember when sending crypto is that you cannot send one cryptocurrency to a different type of cryptocurrency. For example, you cannot send Bitcoin to an Ethereum address. You can only send Bitcoin to a Bitcoin address and Ethereum to an Ethereum address.

So, you now have more information on exchanges and the pros and cons of different exchanges you can use. It's now to move onto trading!

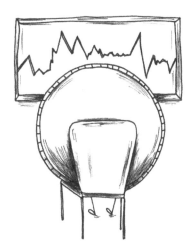

CHAPTER 7:

How to Trade Crypto

Before we discuss in depth the difference in trading platforms, we need to look at the differences between the types of trading you do in active and passive trades and the process you will follow to trade. I will try to use examples where possible to help explain the differences better. Also, in Chapter 13 I outline a 'starter' example crypto trading journey.

Spot, Margin, Perpetual and Futures Trading

Spot trading: In cryptocurrency, spot trading is when you purchase a cryptocurrency, and the transaction executes immediately. You could purchase your chosen crypto with your fiat currency or you could be using one cryptocurrency to buy a different type of cryptocurrency. In whichever way you purchase your crypto, it is the action of buying it and the transaction happening straightaway that defines spot buying. When you passively trade you are spot buying because you are buying that crypto asset at that specific market price with no leverage or margin.

For example: I have £100 and I want to buy £100 worth of Bitcoin. As soon as I press buy on my chosen exchange, that transaction will execute, and I will buy £100 of Bitcoin at whatever the price of Bitcoin is at that specific second.

Margin or leverage trading: This is when you are buying a cryptocurrency by borrowing a certain amount from the trading platform. We will discuss leverage trading in more detail in Chapter 10 but this type of trading is part of active trading. Some trading platforms allow you to borrow up to 100x the amount you have in your wallet. This would mean if you had £1,000 in your wallet, you could technically trade a position on 100x, worth £100,000. Clearly, leverage at that level can carry considerable risks if you are not highly experienced, so I would urge beginners to only trade with 1-2x leverage.

For example: I have £100 but I want to buy £200 of Bitcoin. In order to do this, I need to use a trading platform that allows me to trade with leverage. This is discussed in detail in Chapter 10.

A perpetual contract: This is a special type of futures contract, but unlike the traditional form of futures (see below), it does not have an expiry date, so you can hold a position for as long as you like. Perpetual contracts are often traded at a price that is equal or similar to spot markets. This takes some getting your head around, so here is an illustrative example. For example: I have £100 and I agree to purchase £100 worth of Bitcoin at a buy-in price that I nominate. It may be that the price is currently £x but I only want to buy if the price falls to £x minus $200. If the market moves to a point where this price has been reached, the trade then becomes active and I will have "bought in" or opened a position. It may sound confusing having a few different terms for the same process, but you will often see traders refer to a "buy in" or "opening a position". This just means they are making a trade and buying that crypto at their chosen price point.

Once I have an active trade in the market, this means the price I wanted to buy in at has hit, my perpetual contract is then open. It will remain active and open until it reaches the price I choose to sell the trade at. When you sell a trade, this can also be referred to as closing that position or trade because you are selling and therefore ending the contract you had open.

I do not close the trade, so it could theoretically stay open forever although you pay a fee every day, sometimes twice a day depending on the trading platform, to keep a perpetual trade open. These fees rack up if you have a trade open for a long time. The only other way a trade can end without you telling it to is if you get liquidated. We talk about this in great detail in a few chapters time but being liquidated is when the trading platform closes the trade automatically for you, at a loss, because the market has gone in the opposite direction to your trade. We will talk about this more later, but perpetual contracts are what we normally trade when we actively day trade.

A futures contract: This is an agreement to either buy or sell an asset on a predetermined date, at a pre-established price. Compared to spot trading or simply trading perpetually, futures trading has an expiry date and therefore your crypto must be sold on that pre-determined date at the price agreed.

For example: I have £100 and I purchase £100 of Bitcoin at my chosen buy-in price. Once that trade becomes active, the trade will usually expire on the last Friday of every month. This means the trade will automatically close on that date at the futures price that Bitcoin is showing on that day regardless of whether I am in profit or at a loss. There is a section on Futures Trading further on in this book, with a clear example of how it works.

The 50/50 Rule

The 50/50 rule is a popular trading position used when a trader wants to invest both for the short term and the long term. Short-term trading is what I refer to as active trading and long-term trading is passive trading. The 50/50 rule relates to your likely initial investment in cryptocurrency. When you are starting out, everything is new and you are constantly learning what type of trading you would like to do, which coins and crypto technology you may favour, and so on. There are so many aspects to consider, as we are showing you! As a result, for your first trades, it would be foolish to invest your entire initial stake in just a short-term or just a long-term holding.

This is why many traders like to split their initial investment in half and use 50% of it to buy crypto to hold for the long term and then use the other 50% to buy crypto for daily trading purposes. By splitting your initial investment, you are also mitigating your risk. Let's say, for example, you completely nuke yourself and lose everything in your daily trading pot. You will then still have crypto in your passive trading account. You then have the option to move some of this across into your active trading account to start again. Then when you have built up your active account again you can move some back to your passive pot.

As I mentioned before, I started my crypto journey with £1,000. I split this in half and used £500 to purchase various cryptocurrencies to hold in my portfolio for the long term and £500 to use for active day trading.

You do not need to have a certain amount of money to start trading. You could start with just £10 if you wanted to, but for the sake of consistency in our examples, if I had £100 to invest in crypto, I would split it in half and put £50 in long-term holding and £50 for active trading.

Trading Platforms

A trading platform is a place where you can trade your crypto once it has been converted from fiat and deposited in your trading account. Now, there are various platforms that trade in different ways, and when I talk about trading platforms this is where active trading comes into play.

Active trading is when we are trading in such a way that we are either using leverage (borrowing from the trading platform) or are undertaking trades that need to be watched. Active trading is ideal for quick in-and-out trades or trades where you don't plan on holding that specific currency for a long time.

A point to note about currency terms. You will see that many of the trading exchanges show the fiat as being the US dollar and the price of the crypto asset in US dollars. When trading here in the UK (or from any non-US dollar currency) this can initially be a little confusing. However, your brain does become accustomed to thinking of Bitcoin and other crypto in US dollars. Instead of constantly converting all these numbers back into GB Pounds, I find it best to just have in mind a broad exchange conversion and just get into the flow of trading at a US dollar rate. Of course, you can use the internet to convert the figures back precisely to your fiat if that is more reassuring.

You can undertake passive trading on a trading platform. As a reminder, passive trading is where you buy in at one price and then hold it, choosing to sell when it reaches your desired price point. However, fees can be high so using an exchange rather than a trading platform may be better for passive trading.

A note on trading fees: as with most financial transactions, each time you trade, you need to pay a fee. This is generally at a level of 1-3% on exchanges and between 0.25%-0.75% on trading platforms. The fees you pay also depend on which cryptocurrency you are buying and selling. For example, Ethereum is known for its high transaction fees of around $20 per transaction compared to Litecoin which is around $0.019. Again, these fees change every day and it isn't until you go to make a transaction that you find out the exact level of fee. When you passively trade you pay a fee to buy and then again when you sell your asset. When you actively trade you not only pay a fee to buy, but you also incur a running fee that increases the longer that trade is open. And then, finally, you also pay a fee when you sell.

As mentioned, fees vary per trading platform and cryptocurrency purchased, but for the purpose of an example:

If I wish to open a trade in Bitcoin worth £100. It could cost between 0.25% – 0.75% of that £100 to open the trade. If that trade was open for 1 day you could expect to pay around 3% in open trading fees and then when the trade is sold and closed you would again pay between 0.25%-0.75%.

This means your fees could be around 3.5%-5% in total across the duration of that trade, which in relation to our £100 example would be between £3.50-£5.00. You need to factor this cost into your profit decisions to ensure that when you sell a trade you cover your fees and make a profit on top.

We have talked about the idea of splitting your initial crypto investment in half and using 50% to purchase cryptocurrency to hold for a certain amount of time and then 50% to actively trade with. This means you use half of your investment to trade frequently to make more money, rather than just buying and holding crypto assets and waiting months or even years for them to go up.

It is on active trading platforms that we can use the 50% of our crypto stack to trade every day, or as frequently as we wish, to increase our portfolio. It is active trading, which, for me, is the fun side of crypto. I have made the decision to set aside part of each day to crypto trading as it is only by immersing myself in it in this way and constantly learning about the market and what works and what doesn't work that I have been able to become a successful trader in crypto. You will need to make your own decision about how actively you want to get involved, but hopefully, if you have picked up this book, it is something you are actively considering.

Every aspect of successful active crypto trading is a huge topic and is in fact more than can be shown in a book like this. The best way to learn is to do so via a more visual environment such as an online course, but we will discuss what each trading platform offers.

Here are some of the main trading platforms. Some of these only offer trading in an active format; so, you cannot conduct passive trading on these. There are also some trading platforms that cannot be accessed from certain countries or states. I have listed below some pros and cons for the top trading platforms which I have used. However, as I am based in the United Kingdom, I can only access some of the platforms. For example, I do know that the trading platforms BitSeven and ByBit are popular with US/Australian traders and yet I cannot access these. You will need to check what platforms are available in your country and location.

BitMEX

BitMEX is owned by HDR Global Trading Limited and was founded in 2014. It is a derivative trading platform and is the world's most advanced P2P (Peer to Peer) network only using Bitcoin. This means that even though you are trading in other crypto coins, you buy and sell them using Bitcoin.

In 2020, BitMEX hit the crypto headlines by introducing Know Your Customer (KYC) registration, which required its customers to ID verify themselves and provide their location, instead of just signing up with an email address. This meant that, due to regulations and different state laws, BitMEX suspended their services to customers in restricted locations. As a result, BitMEX is not authorised by the Commodities Futures Trading Commission (CFTC); without a licence their services cannot be used legally in certain locations, such as the United States and some provinces in Canada.

BitMEX is the trading site that I prefer to use; however, which trading site you use comes down to personal preference, as well as your location in the world. You will only develop a preference for a trading site by trying out a few of them and seeing which interface you feel comfortable using. For me, I liked how I could pick and choose which charts and graphs I wanted on BitMex to make it look easier on the eye. I also like that you have the option to trade up to 100x leverage – even though that scale of leveraging isn't recommended, it's nice to have the option. They also process funds quickly and have excellent, helpful customer service, so if you have any issues or problems, they can help resolve them normally within 24 hours. BitMEX can seem complicated and confusing for first-time traders though, in which case Crypto.com or Binance may be preferable when you first start trading.

Pros:

- Has a lot more movement and 'scam wicks.' These are market movements that are excessively high or low and are often not representative of the exact real-time market price.
- Has the option to use 100x leverage on a trade. For example, if I had £100 and used 100x leverage I could trade a position worth £100,000.
- Has cleaned up its platform a lot through KYC registration (more on this below)
- Excellent customer support
- Is easy to navigate once you get used to it

Cons:

- Not easy for beginners until you remove some of the charts and notification boxes
- Has higher fees than most trading platforms
- Is not available for US residents and some other countries

- You can only withdraw from the platform once a day at its designated specific time, and transactions can then take hours, sometimes even a day or two, to reach your account. (This can be annoying if you need to access and withdraw your Bitcoin quickly).

Coinbase Pro

As opposed to the standard Coinbase platform, Coinbase Pro is more advanced and offers the ability to actively trade both with spot and leverage positions. I have used Coinbase Pro but have decided not to keep actively trading on it as I found it hard work, both to understand and just aesthetically it didn't appeal to me.

Pros:

- You can margin/leverage trade
- There are a few more cryptocurrencies available to trade than on Coinbase

Cons:

- Less friendly interface, looks more intense and can be confusing for first time traders
- More suited for intermediary or advanced traders if you can get used to the aesthetics

The exchanges we have mentioned above – Crypto.com, Kraken Pro, Binance, BitSeven and ByBit – are also trading platforms. However, I have not used them to trade so I cannot comment on how well they work for this. Having said that, I have used Crypto.com, Binance and Kraken as exchanges for spot buying and converting my fiat into crypto and found them easy to use and simple enough to understand. I would expect their trading platforms, albeit slightly more advanced, to also show this level of user-friendliness.

Futures Trading

Trading futures is something I have yet to embark upon with my own cryptocurrency journey. Currently I follow the 50/50 rule and have 50% of my starting balance holding crypto assets for the long term and 50% in my active daily trading account. Trading in futures is different to either of these. Cryptocurrency futures are derivative products. A derivative is a financial security whose value is reliant upon or derived from an underlying asset or group of assets. This means the derivative is a contract between two or more parties, and the price of this contract derives from fluctuations in the underlying asset.

Broken down, this means that a futures contract is a commitment between two parties to either buy or sell an asset on a predetermined date, usually at the end of each month, and at a pre-established price. Compared to spot trading or simply trading perpetually without a 'cut-off' date, futures trading has an expiry date and therefore your crypto must be sold on that pre-determined date at the price agreed.

On some trading platforms, with Binance being one of the most popular for futures trading, you would buy your crypto asset and then it will be sold when those purchased contracts expire. Some trading platforms also allow you to leverage trade on futures contacts but, as stated above, I have yet to delve into this type of trading.

Whilst trading futures is probably a less risky and more cost-effective way to trade long term, as there are little-to-no fees on them, I personally feel that establishing an understanding of perpetual contracts and spot buying first will make it easier to get into futures contracts later. However, here is an example of how trading in futures works without using any leverage, just spot buying.

Let's say I have £100 worth of a cryptocurrency that is currently trading at £100 in value. I then take the view that this specific cryptocurrency is going to be worth £200 by the end of the month when the futures contract expires. If the price increases by the time the contract expires,

I will have made £100 profit, but if the price of that crypto has fallen to say £50, I will have lost £50. Basically, you need to be confident that the market is going to continue to rise during that month to enter into some futures trading.

Regulatory updates

At the time of writing, (January 2021), there are a few recent updates to the cryptocurrency market. These updates are to do with security and data sharing on the part of the customer with trading platforms and new regulations within the United Kingdom. The two main changes are to do with KYC registration and the Financial Conduct Authority in the UK.

KYC – Know Your Customer

KYC stands for Know Your Customer, and sometimes Know Your Client. It is a process that has been used within the banking industry for years and is an automatic process we go through without really thinking about. It is basically the process of verifying the identity of a customer to ensure that the person opening the new account is who they claim to be. Banks and other institutions within the financial industry must carry out and comply with these verification processes to help prevent and identify money laundering, corruption and illegal activity. The KYC process involves the customer providing a copy of their ID, (usually a copy of their passport or drivers' licence), face verification using a smartphone camera, and sometimes document verification such as a bank statement or utility bill; this requirement is not considered unusual in certain aspects of everyday life.

One of the main initial attractions of cryptocurrency was its decentralisation and anonymity. However, by their nature, these features can allow scope for illicit activities. This structural inability to 'control and regulate' cryptocurrencies has raised speculation and negativity towards them within the centralised banking system. In 2020, regulations to extend the scope of anti-money laundering (AML) measures to include virtual currency exchange platforms were imposed by world governments. It was announced that KYC would need to be completed on cryptocurrency exchanges and on trading platforms where only an email address was previously required to register.

Whilst most countries have not clearly determined the legality of cryptocurrency, preferring to take a 'wait-and-see' approach, some have set regulations and others have an outright ban. Therefore, the requirement for an exchange/platform to establish the location of their customers has resulted in the suspension of service to those customers in restricted areas. For example, as mentioned previously, this has led to the suspension of service by BitMEX to customers in the United States. For BitMEX to ensure that they are KYC compliant, they ask for permission to locate the device you are signing in from. This enables them to see where in the world you are claiming to be trading from and helps to safeguard them from institutional and authority crackdowns.

Whilst KYC registration has disgruntled some traders, it is a positive thing for the cryptocurrency industry as a whole because it shows how it is becoming more in line with mainstream financial services. This will also lead to the demise of the association with crypto and illicit activity.

The United Kingdom and the FCA

The Financial Conduct Authority (FCA) is an independent, publicly funded body responsible for regulating the financial sector within the UK. Covering nearly 60,000 service providers, they work with consumer groups, trade associations and professional bodies, domestic regulators, EU legislators and a wide range of other stakeholders to ensure markets work well, competitively and fairly for the benefit of customers, staff and shareholders.

However, the FCA does not provide consumer protection powers for the crypto asset activities of firms. Therefore, as cryptocurrency has the potential to be used as a platform to conduct financial crime (such as scamming people, hacking and stealing funds and money laundering), in October 2020 the FCA published rules banning the sale to retail customers of derivatives and exchange traded notes (ETNs) that reference certain types of crypto assets. It has considered that these products are "ill-suited for retail consumers to reliably value" due to cryptocurrency being unregulated, volatile and, in their opinion, lacking legitimate investment need.

This ban implies that retail customers in the UK are incapable of evaluating their own risk and need to be 'protected from themselves'. I can understand the need to protect people from scams; if someone calls you or sends you an email saying, "Send me one bitcoin and I'll give you a million pounds," then alarm bells should be ringing. I can see how the industry can dupe some people, causing them to lose money, and in this book I do not hide the risks and volatility that trading in the cryptocurrency world can involve. However, if you take a sensible approach to trading, gain experience using the desire for knowledge and personal growth that led you to this book in the first place, the opportunity exists to learn to evaluate risk and balance it with profitable outcome.

Whilst many traders thought that their trading and crypto investment days were over when the FCA ruling was issued, this FCA 'ban' is on companies registered in the UK from selling certain types of crypto assets rather than on individuals living in the UK from buying them.

Therefore, as long as you are on a platform which is not registered in the UK you are fine to continue on the basis of your own due diligence, which should be the case anyway. Trading on a platform that is not registered in the UK is not illegal. I cannot stress that enough – it is perfectly legal to buy and trade crypto if you live in the UK; you simply can no longer purchase it from a UK registered platform/business. Fortunately for us the main crypto trading platforms/exchanges, such as Binance and BitMEX, are not registered or based in the UK and can continue to be used.

I have noticed that, since this ban came into effect on the 6 January 2021, there is now a legal notice displayed on BitMEX's site which basically says, "Trade at your own risk from the UK as your money isn't covered or protected by the FCA". This was in fact understood before the 'ban' anyway, so it is nothing new.

Cryptocurrency Scams

As with traditional fiat currency, where money is involved you will find criminals and devious characters. Unfortunately, crypto is no different. In fact, as it is not regulated or protected by any kind of institution, the chances of you seeing a crypto scam or scammer along your new internet journey is highly likely.

Some people take advantage of the fact that crypto is only in its early adoption stages into our society. Common scams you will see are:

- People asking you to send them crypto or money in exchange for more crypto/money.
- People pretending to be certain crypto influencers to earn trust and then ask for money/crypto.
- Fake exchanges and online websites offering you 'amazing' conversion prices if you give them your credit card details/ send them money.
- Fake Instagram, Facebook, Telegram, Discord, WhatsApp groups, all set up to try and convince you to send them money.
- Fake courses promising to teach you how to earn £5 million in a week if you send them some bitcoin.

The moral of the story with crypto scams is:

— **NEVER** send anyone your crypto currency or your money.

— Always check when signing up to an exchange or trading platform that it is their legitimate website.

— Don't use exchanges/trading platforms that have no reputation or are small.

— Always research extensively if you choose to sign up for a crypto trading course. Read reviews, find their social media, find out as much as you can and try to speak to students who have taken their course. Any legitimate trading course will be more than happy to answer questions.

— Never accept friend requests online from people saying they can help you to make money with crypto. Also bear in mind that no legitimate person or company will reach out to you and ask you to send them money to trade with.

— Protect yourself and your cryptocurrency at all times!

CHAPTER 8:

Technical Analysis and Trading Types

Having discussed and explained the initial set-up process of finding an exchange and a trading platform that you enjoy using, we can start to delve a little deeper into what you are looking at on your screen once you are all KYC registered and set up. This chapter is going to run through the next stages and look at new aspects of trading cryptocurrency. As I have mentioned before, this book has been designed to be an introduction into the basics of cryptocurrency on a broad spectrum and this is why there are certain elements that we cover and explain but only at a surface level. There is always more to learn; I would encourage anyone who is interested in a deeper level of technical analysis and trading to continue their research.

When I first began wanting to learn more about this sector, I took part in a few online classes. The great thing with these is that they allow you to visually see and learn about what is happening on a trading platform. I am a very visual person, so I respond and learn more when I can both read about and see illustrations of what I am studying.

Unfortunately, as in many other areas, there are courses out there which are scams that will take your money but not teach you anything. So, before signing up to one it is important to research them and look in detail at the person or company selling the class. Look at all their social media – do they have reviews? Can you purchase the course on a credit card so that you have protective cover if it isn't legitimate? Who knows, one day I may create my own course, which I promise will be what it says it is on the tin! But until that time, there is a vast array of free resource crypto material available online, such as articles and how-to videos on YouTube. In such a fast-moving world, it is not surprising that there are various news sites on all things crypto. A couple of good examples of this are *Coin Telegraph* at cointelegraph.com, and *The Daily Hodl* at dailyhodl.com – no, I've not spelt that incorrectly – we will talk about hodling in Chapter 12.

Immerse yourself in the crypto world. I have created a social media account on Instagram just for crypto (feel free to follow me @ cryptocountess), so that I can follow and absorb information from crypto influencers, crypto news and other traders. You will be surprised how much free information is out there when it comes to learning how to read a chart or complete a certain action on a trading website. By surrounding yourself with information on what you want to learn it becomes familiar and easier for your brain to absorb.

When you first start looking at using a trading platform, the primary thing to remember is that it is not necessary for you to understand everything on it. Every trading platform has its own trading indicators, which are specific trading elements that you can add into the normal market chart. You may not ever understand everything on there, and you certainly won't use every single indicator, but once you are confident with the basics you will feel ready to start trading.

Technical Analysis

To begin with we are going to explain and look at technical analysis (TA). By definition, TA is a trading discipline used every day by stock market traders to evaluate investments and identify trading opportunities in price trends and patterns seen on charts. Many who use TA do so because they believe that analysing past trading activity and price points can help guesstimate where future prices could go. It is most common within stocks, futures, commodities, fixed income, currencies and other securities, although there are some traders who believe that TA can be used within crypto.

However, there is a strong divide within the cryptocurrency world over whether it can or should be used when looking at the crypto market, which is far more volatile than the stock market. Some have the viewpoint that, because crypto is so volatile, you shouldn't waste time trying to over-analyse what has happened and whether that price event may happen again but just trade what you see on any given day. Others believe that looking at what crypto has done, or how much is being moved in or out of an exchange, will help you to decide where the market is moving.

A theory that was once pointed out to me on a crypto forum was that, even if you don't believe that TA works in cryptocurrency, if you have a group of people that are all looking at the same chart and all come to the same conclusion that this price is the bottom and this price is the top, then TA forms naturally because those automatically become resistance and support levels – we will be explaining these terms shortly. This makes sense but also reinforces the point that trading what you see with crypto is more often than not the best way to take advantage of the market at that specific time.

Whilst I do not currently have the interest or desire to really learn TA in depth, there are a few key things which you should know and understand when looking at a chart as a beginner. The core elements of TA that we will be explaining at a beginner level are candlesticks, candlestick timeframes, support and resistance levels, and the money flow indicator (MFI).

First, it is important to understand that in trading you have two types of trading personalities, the bears and the bulls. These terms are commonly used in the stock market and are also used in crypto.

A bull is a trader who prefers to long, they want to push the price up, they believe in upward trends and they buy during the dips in price action to accumulate more of an asset. This means that when there is a crash, or a bull believes price action is at the bottom of its current range, they buy in the hope the price will shortly be increasing.

A bear is a trader who prefers to short, they want to sink the price of an asset and enjoy seeing downward trends. They buy at the top of a price point so that they can ride the wave down. I explain trading long and short in the next chapter, along with helping you to be clearer on why someone would want the price to fall on an asset they have bought – this has taken me a while to get my head around!

Most traders can be identified as either a bear or a bull. If you see the term permabull or permabear, it means that they tend to only trade in one direction and will not switch. However, there are some traders who trade the trend, which is what I do, not classifying myself as either a bull or a bear. I am whichever type of trader I need to be on that day to enter and close a position in profit. I feel that any long-term, successful trader should be both a bull and a bear, as trading in only one specific direction means that you will not be taking advantage of all price movements, and therefore you are missing out on maximizing profits.

You will often see the two types of trader on cryptocurrency forums, throwing abuse or banter at one another. It is often quite childish and totally irrelevant to the point of trading, but it is interesting to see their opinions on why they believe a crypto asset is going to move in a specific direction.

As well as there being a bull versus bear culture within trading there are also specific strategies used depending on personal style and risk allowance. There are five commonly recognised types of traders: scalpers, swing traders, day traders, momentum traders and position trading.

Scalping

A scalper is a type of trader who specialises in making and taking profits from small price movements. They make quick, small trades every day which means they could trade anywhere from 2-100 times a day if they wished. Scalping involves being in and out of a trade quickly and taking advantage of small price actions. It is most common to scalp trade on the 1-minute or 3-minute chart, we will go into more detail what these charts are in the next chapter, and they tend to take profits within seconds or minutes. Scalp trading can be fun, as you take profits quickly; however, it is not for beginners! It requires a sound understanding of charts and price movements, and it is intense as you need to be watching your computer at all times and is really only a style that can be used by a full-time trader.

Swing Trading

A swing trader is a someone who trades on a slightly longer timeframe than a scalper and often has a trade open for one to seven days. They take advantage of a short-term trend and either ride the wave up or down depending on their preference. This style of trading is less intensive and allows someone to trade part-time. With swing trading you can enter at your chosen price point and then set an exit and just walk away and wait for it to hit. No or low leverage is best, to avoid any liquidations if there is a market movement in the opposite direction to your trade. As you are not watching it constantly, you need to have peace of mind when swing trading and know that your trade is safe to run its course.

Day Trading

A day trader, as the name suggests, is someone who buys and sells their asset on the same day. A day trade will be held from a few minutes to a few hours but will be closed by the end of their day. Unlike the stock market, where there is a specific closing time each day, cryptocurrency is open for trading 24/7. This means that day traders within cryptocurrency ensure they have no overnight positions open and aim to enter and exit the same day within their relevant time zone.

Scalping and day trading are the most time-critical trading strategies and require the most commitment. They are both full-time trading styles and require a strong risk management strategy to minimise any losses resulting from market trend changes. So, not for the faint-hearted!

Momentum Trading

Momentum trading occurs when a trader notices that a particular asset is "breaking out." This could either be up or down, depending on how the trader likes to trend trade, but when it breaks out the trader jumps in to ride it up or down. These trades typically last for a few hours or days depending on how much volume there is. Momentum traders are often seen as the "fomo-ers" (fear of missing out) of trading because they are jumping on a fast-moving train to try to capture quick profits.

Position Trading

Position traders, otherwise known as long term traders, are people who stay in a trade for weeks or months. They are not concerned about short-term price fluctuations because they believe their investment will be profitable in the long term. This kind of trading is best done with no leverage, so you are literally buying at one price and then selling at another in the future. Long term traders are the most patient and this style works best for people who have little time to focus on their trading.

The beauty of all these trading styles is that you don't have to pick one specific style and stick to it. You can be any style of trader you wish on any given day. I enjoy scalp trading when I have plenty of time, but I also do swing trades on days where I can't check my computer every hour. Having spot-bought cryptocurrency (bought at one price with no leverage), to hold for the next few years also makes me a position trader as well.

Trading holds many possibilities for all types of personalities, so whilst you may find that one suits you and your lifestyle more than another, you have freedom of choice. It is also the case that the more experience you gain, the more you move into these different styles of trading. In the next chapter we will look at charts in more detail and explain about candlestick patterns.

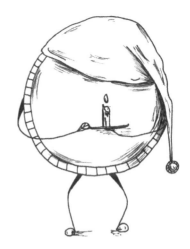

CHAPTER 9:

Candlesticks and Charting

Having looked at the different types of traders we can now delve a little deeper into the different types of technical analysis (TA) that we can use initially to better understand when or when not to trade. As mentioned previously, the main TA indicators that we are going to focus on are candlesticks, charting patterns, long and short days, resistance and support levels and the money flow indicator (MFI).

Candlesticks

In trading, whether it is trading the stock market or cryptocurrency, candlestick charts are a TA tool used to look at the market price. These candlesticks can be viewed in various time frames and patterns in trying to gauge which direction the market is moving.

Candlestick charts date back to 18th century Japanese rice traders, where they would use them to track market prices and daily momentum for rice purchases. These candlestick charts were then brought to the West by Steve Nison in 1991. Nison wrote a book called *Japanese Candlestick Charting Techniques*, which has helped many traders to identify dozens of patterns. Candlestick formations are a critical TA tool for many traders. On most trading exchanges now, the candlestick colours are green and red, with green indicating a rise in market price and red indicating a fall. Images (1) and (2) show representative green and red candlesticks.

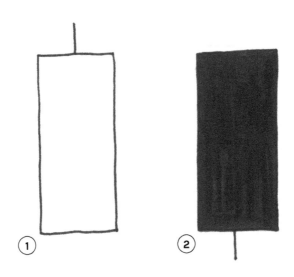

Due to the fact this book is not printed in colour the white candles represent what would be green, long upward trend movements. The black candles represent red, short downward trend candles.

The white candle represents a strong, green, upward candle. (Image 1).
The black candle represents a strong, red, downward candle. (Image 2)

Understanding the different lengths of a candle and what certain candles mean is an important part of learning to trade. However, if you decide to delve into the meanings of exact candlestick formations then I would recommend independently researching this specific technical tool.

There are multiple candlestick patterns with individual names that can be used in reaching a decision to trade. However, this level of detail can hinder you if you are too caught up looking for a particular candlestick formation or chart pattern and then you completely miss a good entry point. For initial trading they aren't necessary. I still don't over complicate what I know about candlestick patterns and I just stick to the simple analysis of looking for 'tops and bottoms' to enter.

Long & Short Positions

When trading there are two directions you can trade. To trade 'long' is to bet in the sense that you think the trend is going up; this is referred to as the green direction. To trade 'short' is to bet that you think the market trend is going down; this is referred to as the red direction.

A green day would be represented by multiple green candles forming an upward trend. This would indicate that the market was full of buyers, which pushes the price higher and higher. A red day is recognised by multiple red candles forming a downward trend, indicating that the market is full of sellers. When there is a strong sell-off the price can dramatically drop. This action causing a decrease in price is in fact not a negative because the lower the market price falls for a certain cryptocurrency, the more it will attract buyers who want to buy in at a lower price.

One thing I really struggled with when I first started learning about crypto trading was the whole aspect of shorting. I understood that if you bought in at a low price and "bet" that it would be going up, so you entered long, then you would obviously make money when that asset reached a higher price point and you sold.

For the purposes of an example let's assume that you have 1 whole Bitcoin to trade. If I entered a long trade and the price of that Bitcoin was at £4,500 and it went up to £5,000 and I sold, I would make a profit of £500.

But it took my brain longer to grasp the concept of making money when the market is going down. One day it did just click, so I hope my explanation will help that happen sooner for you.

On a trading platform you have a green button for buying and a red button for selling. When you long, you buy at the bottom and sell at the top, so you press the green button to buy and then the red button to sell at a higher price. When you short you do the opposite; you press the red button to sell and then the green button to buy at a lower price.

By definition, going short on a trade is when you "sell" a set value of contracts and then "buy" them back when the asset has fallen to your desired level. This sell and then buy concept is what sent my brain into a crazy "what???" state. I think the use of sell and buy as an opposite was one of the reasons why I struggled to grasp this to start off with, so let's break it down further to explain how shorting works. It is the opposite of deciding to make a long trade, where you enter and buy at a low price and then sell at a higher price to make profit. Deciding to make a short trade is where you enter at a high price in the hope that you think the price is going to drop and go down. In order to enter a short trade, you are buying high and selling low but you use the opposite buttons on a trading platform to do this:

To go long: you press the buy button to enter the trade and then the sell button to exit that trade.

To go short: you press the sell button to enter the trade and then the buy button to exit that trade.

Let's use the example of the long trade from before. The cryptocurrency I was trading is now at £5,000 and I think it is now going to go back down. I would enter a short trade to sell 1 whole Bitcoin at £5,000 and the price then drops to £4,500. I can then buy back 1 whole Bitcoin at £4,500 and have made a £500 profit from the difference.

I know this may all seem a huge amount to get your head around, particularly the whole idea of being keen for a price to drop, and trust me it took me several weeks to really get my head around shorting, but I promise you will get it. It will probably click more for you when you are actually looking at a trading platform and can visualise and see in front of you what I have described. I would definitely use this page as a reference point when you are first getting to grips with your trading platform.

When there is a significant price drop it can lead to a rapid price increase, as people rush to buy back in and demand exceeds supply. Remember, what goes up is likely to come down and vice versa! It is important to know that not all cryptocurrencies move together – in fact some move against one another. For example, Bitcoin may be going up one day whilst other cryptocurrencies will be going down. This tends to happen when traders "pull profits" from one coin to put into another.

Even though there are two directions you can trade, a no trading candle will help to determine an 'iffy' market, indicating that trading should be avoided for that day. These days are called no trading zones and often occur after a big crash or upward spike, when the bears and bulls are unsure as to where the market will go. Indecision between the two causes the direction of the candlesticks to look like crosses as per image (overleaf). When you see one of these candles I would refrain from trading until a clearer market direction shows itself.

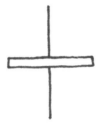

(as it is referred to further on): Image 3: This candle represents what we call a no trading day or an indecisive candle.

Candlestick Timescales

The trading platform you decide to use will determine what indicators are available to you, as each platform is different. However, most of them all have the following candlestick charts available:

1 minute, 3 minutes, 5 minutes, 15 minutes, 30 minutes, 1 hour, 2 hours, 3 hours, 4 hours, 6 hours, 12 hours, 1 day, 3 days, 1 week, 2 weeks and 1 month.

As you learn and become more comfortable with the platform you have chosen to trade on, you will also have timescales you prefer to look and trade on. My personal preferences have become the 1-minute, the 4-hour and the 6-hour chart. I like to trade the 1-minute chart especially, as I enjoy scalp trading. Whichever candlestick chart you are looking at, each candle represents that selected timescale. For example, each candle on the 1-minute chart represents 1 minute; each candlestick on the 6-hour represents 6 hours. That may seem obvious, but when you are first starting out, looking at these charts can be quite overwhelming and confusing.

Each platform will also have various candlestick chart layouts to choose from. Again, this is a personal preference thing; however, I prefer to look at candlesticks in the Heikin Ashi layout. Heikin Ashi means 'average bar' in Japanese and has a smoother look, essentially taking an average of the movement for each candle formation.

'Normal' candlestick charts, which are often just called candles on a trading platform selection section, alternate between green and red even if the price is moving dominantly in one direction. This makes them harder to follow as I feel they can over-complicate your mind and prevent you from making good trading decisions. By using the Heikin Ashi candlesticks you can eliminate as much chaos from the charts as possible, which makes for a better trading perspective. Again, this is just my opinion, and as you learn more about the tools available on each platform and the cryptocurrency you have chosen to trade, you will make your own decisions.

What is a candlestick wick?

Candlestick wicks are lines that are attached to the body of the candle and can be positive or negative, meaning they can come out from the top of the candle or out from the bottom. The length of the wick shows how high or low the price went on that specific candle movement. They can help to show direction and establish whether it is a good time to enter into a trade or not. We talked previously about scam wicks, when the length of the wick from the candle is excessively long.

Trading Orders & Wicks

When actively trading there are two ways you can enter a trade. Either with a limit order or with a market order and both can be used in long or short trades. A limit order refers to orders placed by traders to buy or sell a cryptocurrency when a certain price is reached. This is in contrast to market orders, where a cryptocurrency is sold or bought at the current best available price.

For example: If a cryptocurrency is currently trading at £100 and you want to enter long but not at the current price. You can place a limit order for say £85 and this will become active if the price drops to this level. The same goes for a short trade. If you think the price might reach £150 before dropping you could place a limit order high on a short trade so once that hits, the hope would be it would then fall and you would make a profit.

Limit orders are a great way of taking advantage of dips and the volatility in the crypto world whereas market orders allow you to enter or exit immediately at whatever the current market price is. It should also be noted that fees on limit orders are less than fees on market orders.

Scam wicks are loved by limit order traders waiting for a good entry but hated by over-leveraged traders because it causes them to be stopped out or liquidated. They can be great for reaching price points that would normally seem to be unreachable at that current market level. An example of candlesticks with long wicks are shown in images (4) and (5)

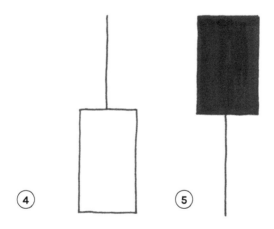

The white candle represents a green candle with a long wick or tail upwards. (Image 4). The black candle represents a red candle with a long wick or tail downwards. (Image 5)

A trader who is over-leveraged is someone who has entered a trade and used too much margin or leverage on that trade, so they are at risk of being liquidated. We discuss in further detail what liquidation and stops are in the next chapter. However, in cryptocurrency trading, liquidation is when an open trade is closed by the trading platform at a certain price point and the value of that position will be removed from your balance. Liquidation happens when the market moves against you to such an extent that you cannot get out of or save the trade. One way of saving some of your balance and preventing yourself from being liquidated is by using a stop loss, otherwise known as a stop order. This is where you choose a certain price point to exit your trade if it is running at a loss. You cut your losses in a sense and even though you will lose a bit of your wallet, "stopping yourself out", which is the phrase traders use, is sometimes the best thing to do to minimise your losses if the market is really going against you. In the next chapter we talk more about the different types of stop orders you can make.

Candlestick Bodies

The length of a candlestick is one of the clearest signs of a trend in a specific direction when looking at a chart. If the candlestick is long in body, then it is strong and the direction it is heading is clear. If it is shorter, then it is losing momentum and the direction may be getting ready to change. Candlesticks that become really thin and start to look like horizontal lines (see image (3), indicate the price is about to change direction or that the market is unsure where it wants to go. This is when the price action can start to consolidate into a range between two price points before a clear direction forms.

Resistance & Support Levels

As with the stock market, every cryptocurrency has what is called resistance and support points. These are created by the bears and the bulls when they either buy or sell the asset.

A resistance point is a certain price point that would be classified as the current top, the maximum that the asset has reached at any specific point. Resistance points get 'tested' by the bulls as they buy and try to push the price up and beyond the resistance point. When this buying power fails, the asset price will drop, and the bears take over. At this point, selling starts and continues until the price falls and reaches what is referred to as its support level.

The support level is, as its name suggests, the point at which multiple previous buyers have entered and prevented the asset price from falling further. The bears try to repeatedly test this level, to break it and push the price down further.

Understanding the current resistance and support levels for any trading chart is important, as it helps you in deciding when to enter a trade. Let's say, for example, that it is a green day, the candles have been strong, and the trend is positively upward. You think you will enter long to take advantage of the increase in price; however, the price is nearing the top of the current resistance. It would not be a good idea to enter a trade at or near the top of current resistance as this could mean you will then get stuck at the top and have to wait for the asset to fall and then come back up again to free you. Longing at the top or shorting at the bottom of resistance and support points are when you are most likely to get into a tricky situation. As a simple motto to remember, to trade successfully we want to **long at the bottom and short at the top**.

Bear Market: A bear market is a situation within the digital currency market defined by caution and hesitation. During a bear market, people are more likely to sell than buy. You can expect to see lower highs and lower lows. It is a sustained period of time, characterised by downward movements.

Bull Market: A bull market is the opposite to a bear market, and is when the market trend is up. This market is full of confidence and optimism and can be seen by a clear growth in the digital currency market.

A Bear Market and a Bull Run

The cryptocurrency market goes through cycles of movement and these range from being in what is called a bear market, a bull run or a flat market.

A bear market is when the overall trend is negative and downward. Whilst there will be upward swings, the general market is controlled by the bears and selling pressure is higher than buying pressure.

A bull run is the opposite and is indicative of a consistent uptrend propelled by excessive buying. Bull runs are exciting because you experience large amounts of price movement and action in a short space of time and these large moves in the market allow for multiple daily trading opportunities. Bull runs are often fuelled by people seeing there is a sudden upward movement, then experiencing FOMO (the fear of missing out), and rush to buy in, which then causes the bull run to increase even further.

A flat market is when there is minimal movement in either direction. On any given day, the price could move only 1-2 dollars compared to a bear or bull run where you can see $100 swings in a day.

Money Flow Indicator

On BitMEX there is an indicator called the MFI or Money Flow Indicator which helps us to view whether the trading pattern is at the top or bottom. Even if you do not trade on BitMEX you can still use their indicator tools to help you make decisions on another exchange.

The image below is an example of what the MFI looks like on BitMEX. When the line is in the lower area at the bottom of the Indicator, this would be a good time to think about entering a long position. When the line can be seen in the upper area above the middle section, this would indicate it would be a good entry point to short.

Now, this being said, if the trend is strongly upward or downward then the MFI must be evaluated for the day trend. It cannot be relied upon to guarantee safety for every entry, but it is a valuable indicator to use. For day trading, I only look at the MFI on the 1-minute chart, as this is when it is most clearly showing entry signs.

However, the MFI on the 6-hour chart can show you if the market is reaching the top or bottom of that specific market movement. If the MFI on the 6-hr is reaching the bottom it indicates that the trend is getting ready to change and reverse, so then you would look at the 1-minute chart for a good entry point. Think of it as moving in to see a magnified view of the chart. Vice versa if the MFI is at the top of the 6-hr, it would indicate we would be going down for a bit of a correction. Sometimes the MFI on the 6-hr can move quickly and other times it can take weeks to go from top to bottom.

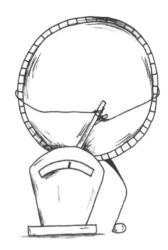

CHAPTER 10:

Leverage Trading and Liquidation

In this chapter we are going to be talking about trading with leverage, and liquidation. Trading with leverage is something that most traders do, either by using a low leverage for minimal risk or a higher leverage if they wish to accept greater risk.

Leverage trading, also referred to as margin trading, is effectively a loan offered by a broker on an exchange during trading to increase the availability of funds in trades. Whilst this can potentially grow your stack quicker than simply buying crypto at one price and selling at another, the higher your leverage, the greater the risk of your being stopped out or liquidated.

For example, you have an account balance of £5 and you want to place a trade with a leverage of 10x. You can then open a position that is worth £50, which means your profit will be 10 times greater. However, if the market moves against you, your losses will also mirror this.

Trading with leverage is a great way to grow your portfolio but as recommended earlier, you should only use low leverage when you first start, i.e. 1-2x. When the market is in a strong position and you know what you are doing you can be more confident with your risk analysis and with this comes an ability to enter into an increase in leverage. I cannot stress enough, however, how important it is to be experienced when using high leverages.

Anything over 10x I would consider to be high risk and is not for the faint-hearted or inexperienced. I can state that I feel it is high risk because I have personally lost a fair sum of money by being silly with my leverage. See, I have made mistakes so you don't have to! I went through a stage for about a week after I had been stopped out from a bull run where I felt pressure to make back my wallet super quick. So, I chose leverage at 25x on everything and hoped for the best. Just like a gambler at the races who has lost a wedge on one race and then places a large stake on a long odds horse in the next race in a desperate bid to recoup losses, I can see now that this was unlikely to end well.

The problem with 25x is that unless you are watching the trade like a hawk and are literally in and out, it can turn on you in a minute and clear out your funds. Whilst choosing higher leverage allows you to bet less of your own money, if the trade turns you can lose funds quicker, even with a stop loss in place. I explain below 'stop loss', or 'stop order' as it is also known. I don't know why I went into this crazy 25x stage. The market was volatile, it wasn't even a good, clear trading period, but I just got caught up in the hype and suffered the consequences.

I am telling you this because while it is easy to say in a completely rational manner, "If you do this and don't do that then you're going to be fine, and you will be the best trader there ever was." As humans, we are ruled by the head... and the heart. We are not computers making clean binary decisions based purely on the data. Emotions such as excitement, greed, anxiety, envy, FOMO, a whole cocktail of complex competing thoughts end up clouding your judgment! That's just life, BUT the important thing is to recognise that you will not always behave rationally in the heat of the trading moment. To be honest, at times that is all part of the fun – the adrenalin rush, the rollercoaster ride, the playing with fire, the thrill of the chase and the pushing the envelope of risk. This thrill may even be the main reason you want to get into crypto trading. However, be aware that taken on in that way, you are entering into it in the same spirit as our racing gambler. You are gambling and you need to set clear parameters on what you are prepared to gamble... and lose.

So, while you may be reading this book and taking on board all the clear guidelines and techniques of trading, you may end up only applying around 10% of the "rules" and then you'll get greedy or over cautious and either go crazy or be too scared to do anything. This happens to everyone, it really does. Some of the best traders I follow now have nearly lost it all; trading can be emotional, and you can get carried away.

It becomes a simple equation: the less detailed analysis you do and the more you let emotions crowd in and cloud your judgment, the more you are crypto gambling. The greater the detailed analysis you conduct, of the type I am outlining in this chapter, and the more you are governed by your head and not your heart, the more you are crypto trading. Before entering a trade, you need to know what price you are happy going in at, so you should know the exact price point you are happy exiting at to make profit, and also how much you are willing to lose if you have to cut and stop yourself out. Knowing this before you enter helps you override the impulsive behaviour that can take over your mindset.

By being honest with my experiences I hope to help you avoid the same mistakes. The temptation to want to earn money fast, especially when you have had a few good trade runs, can take over your brain and make you feel invincible. But you aren't and the market will not always be your friend. At the end of the day, you will become a good trader by losing. You will then become a great trader by learning from those mistakes and getting back in the game. So, keep your leverage low, compound your wins and don't try and ride the buckaroo 50x leverage bull in your first week of trading, if ever!

One of the most common phrases you will come across in the crypto world is people talking about getting REKT (yes spelt like that). People tend to type it in capitals too just to emphasis their position, but it basically means your trade is going to get you liquidated or that you will lose a lot of money on it. For example, when the market starts to pump, which means it experiences a sudden, fast, upward surge, you will see the forums flood with bullish comments about bears getting rekt. The same happens when there is a dump but this time bears say the bulls are all about to get rekt. Most of the time it is just hyping off one another to cause fomo and make people reading it either cancel their trades or try and buy in.

This taunting of rekt is a great example of how freewheeling and combative the world of crypto can be. Bears and bulls can act like fans of opposing football teams, taunting each other and being tribal in their responses. You can weigh in or ignore all this, it's up to you!

As we have mentioned before, successful trading is all about being prepared, analysing the trends, and limiting your exposure and vulnerability to the market. At any moment the market can bounce or dump, causing your trade to suddenly go underwater. By implementing something called a stop order, you can limit how much money you risk losing and avoid liquidation, which in turn saves more of your wallet. A stop order is used to help protect your trades if the market starts to go against you. There are a few different stop orders you can place on your account depending on how you want to exit the trade. You may also hear a stop order referred to as a stop loss, but they are one and the same and just mean you are stopping how much you can lose.

A stop order will be placed when the market reaches the trigger price you set. The trigger price is value you have entered to leave the market at. The stop order will not enter the order book until the market reaches the trigger price. This type of strategy is used two ways:

1. As a risk management tool to limit losses on positions.
2. As an automatic tool to enter the market at a desired entry point without having to manually wait for the market to move to place the order.

As I use BitMEX for trading, I will be talking about the three types of stop orders they offer. Most trading platforms offer similar orders, but I cannot comment on how exactly others work as I don't use them.

The three stop orders available on BitMEX are:

1. Stop-market Order
2. Stop-limit Order
3. Trailing Stop Order

A Stop-Market Order

A stop-market order opens or is triggered when the stop price is hit. In BitMEX you then pay the taker fee of 0.075%. Market orders of any kind are the more expensive out of the two orders, (market and limit), but they are immediately activated and therefore allow you to get out of a trade quickly.

A Stop-Limit Order

A stop-limit order is like a stop-market order, but it allows you to set the price of your order once your stop price is triggered. After the stop price is triggered, the limit order takes effect to ensure that the order is not completed unless the price is at or better than the limit price specified. This can be used by more experienced traders as an alternative to stop-market orders if you wish to control your exit and reduce the taker fee to 0.025%.

A Trailing Stop Order

A trailing stop order is when you place a trailing value on a trade. It is a modification of a market or limit stop order that can be set at a certain percentage or monetary amount away from the current market price. For a long position, you would place a trailing stop loss below the current market price. For a short position, you would place the trailing stop above the current market price.

A trailing stop is designed to protect your gains by enabling a trade to remain open and continue to profit as long as the price is moving in your favour. The trailing stop order closes the trade if the price changes direction by your previously specified percentage or monetary amount.

Using stop orders or stop losses is a good way of protecting your trades if they should suddenly change direction on you. However, it is important to bear in mind that they can also work against you. For example, you are going long, and you entered at £500. If the price starts to drop and you have placed a stop order to close your trade at £480 then you would have lost £20. However, if you are on no or a low leverage then you can afford to let the price drop a bit knowing it will eventually go back up, over your entry price, allowing you to exit in profit.

This is where it is key to have protected yourself with leverage because it gives you the time and breathing space to access your trade and know that you do not need to stop yourself out at a loss.

Stop orders are a great way to ensure that you do not lose too much if you feel you cannot save the trade before it reaches your liquidation. They are not necessary, however, for every trade you make.

Liquidation

Now let's talk liquidation. This is the Voldemort word of the cryptocurrency world! For those of you not familiar with Harry Potter books, Voldemort is the main evil character and you do not say his name unless you want bad things to happen. Liquidation is the same: we don't want to talk about it for fear of putting that worry out there to occur, but at the same time we need to be aware of it and work out how to best to prepare for it.

Liquidation within finance is when the assets of a business are sold to repay creditors before the business closes down. In cryptocurrency trading, liquidation is when an open trade is closed by the exchange at a certain numerical point and the value of that position will be removed from your balance. Liquidation happens when the market moves against you to such an extent that you cannot get out of or save the trade and impending doom is inevitable.

When you initially open a trade position on an exchange, unless you are opening it without using any leverage, you are required to hold a percentage of the total value of that position; this is called the maintenance margin requirement. If a trade starts to go against you and therefore heads towards your liquidation price, if you cannot pad the position up by lowering your leverage and adding more of your balance to the original percentage opened, then liquidation will trigger when it hits that liquidation price. At this point you will then lose the value of your trade in your maintenance margin plus fees. This is shown as your realised profit and loss in your closed position panel. Profit and loss (P&L) are often referred to as PNL and this term will probably appear in your panel.

No one wants to get liquidated, although it is unfortunately one of those tough lessons you will learn the hard way. When you've been liquidated, and I mean properly liquidated and lost maybe as much as a few thousand in one trade, it will sharpen your focus. There are strategies you can implement to try and prevent this from happening, to protect your yield, but sometimes the system just goes against you and there is nothing you can do to fight it. I honestly think everyone will get liquidated at some point. That being said, it is such a heavy lesson to learn that we obviously want to try and avoid it at all cost.

The first time you get liquidated, as to be honest it will probably happen more than once in your trading lifetime, the best thing to do is take a deep breath, have a mini emotional breakdown, dust yourself off and start again. Now when I say start again, I do not mean jump right back in 5 minutes later and open another trade. That would be the worst thing you could do because you are still emotional and running off adrenaline, sadness and frustration. If you get liquidated or even if you close a losing trade using a stop loss, I would strongly suggest that you walk away from the computer for at least 24 hours. Do not try and trade again on the same day, as you need to give your mind some space and time to process what happened and learn from your mistakes. After a liquidation you need to analyse what you have done, where you went wrong and how you can avoid doing that again.

I remember my first close call when I had only been trading for about 2 weeks; I was doing pretty well and feeling a bit over-confident in my ability at the time to read the market. There had just been a Bitcoin halving, (a monumental occurrence that happens every 4 years where the Bitcoin block reward decreases by half), which had pushed the price of Bitcoin up and created massive volatility in the market. This led me to get a bit over-excited and I was just bumbling along going "Trade! Trade! Trade!". I saw that the market was fluctuating between two price points on the chart, so I decided to place four long trades, close in price, across all four of my BitMEX accounts. In hindsight I would never do that now, use all four accounts up on a similar trade entry price, but I was foolish then! The market came down and filled all my orders, I thought, "Great, here we go, time for the market to now move back up and I will then be in profit on all four accounts!" This was what I wanted, buy in cheaper and ride the wave back up again. The problem was that it didn't go back up. It went down. Way, way down. It dropped over 10% in the space of a few hours and I just had to sit and watch myself sink into trade debt.

It was emotional and not something I enjoyed experiencing; however, I needed to try and chase down my liquidation prices. The only problem was I didn't have much padding in my account and had also added leverages of 10-25%. Not a good plan! I didn't want to have to put money into the accounts as I was quite firm that I had wanted to start with a certain amount and trade myself up. So, I came to the realisation that it was likely I was going to get liquidated and if it happened, I decided I would be okay with that. In fact, as it turned out, that time I just avoided it, but it was so close, like sweaty hands and feet close, and was not a pleasant experience.

The first time I got liquidated was for £638. I had made around £3,500 profit by this point and had been trading properly for a few weeks. I had two of my accounts set to short, again in hindsight I now don't have multiple accounts doing the same thing, but I thought I was confidently shorting the top of an Ethereum pump. But it wasn't the top, and in fact there was then a super quick pump up by another 6%. One of my accounts with the short on had a long liquidation price, so it was far away.

Everyone's idea of where they feel comfortable with their liquidation price is different but at this time, it was around April/May 2020, and on this account, I had entered a trade when Ethereum was trading at around £200, and my liquidation was around £220. I was most definitely on a higher leverage amount than I should have been, at the time it was around 10x, but Ethereum was only really moving up and down between £5-£10 daily at the time so I thought I was safe. I don't know why, but for some reason I wasn't on it and I didn't check my other account before I went to sleep to see what the liquidation price was against my leverage. I then woke up the following morning to find that I had been liquidated on the account that I hadn't checked. It turns out I had entered a little lower on the second account but as my leverage was still high, my liquidation was at £210 and it hit that on the overnight pump. Looking back on it I was crazy to be on such high leverage because now I know as of March 2021, we can get dips and pumps that range between £1,000-£3,000 in an hour! But back then we weren't in a bull market and I had no idea what was in store!

At first, I was in denial. I didn't want to tell anyone. I had been eager to share the news of my wins with my family and my partner but when I had my first loss, I felt quite ashamed. Now, in comparison to what I had gained at that point, the loss wasn't that great – I was still up by just under £3000. But who likes to lose money? No one! I did wallow for a couple of hours, felt super deflated and started to wonder whether I should just bail out. Remember, at this point I was still in another short on another account and the market was still going in the opposite direction so the fear of having a double liquidation was quite real! As I say, I wallowed for a few hours, had a little nap and then thought, you know what, if I can't accept the loss then I don't deserve the gains. So, I got up, made a caramel mocha and sat down to re-assess what I could do to rectify the situation and claw back my losses. I made a plan that the next day I would place new limit orders to start entering some small trades. Sometimes after a big loss you need to take baby steps again to build up your confidence and make sure you are following the trading steps properly. I also decided to always keep two trading accounts free from trades so they can go the opposite way to any trade I might get stuck in. That way if I am making a loss on one account, I can make a win on another.

The only time it is good to have two accounts in the same position, for example they are both in long positions, is if your entry price is dramatically different. Let us say the market moves against your original position and drops by 5%. When the candles stop dropping and it looks like it is stabilising and has reached the bottom of the dip, then you can re-enter long as the trading chart starts to move up again. This way even though you are in two long positions, one is earning money as it goes back up to reach your other one.

Here is an example of this using our £100:

On account 1 we have entered a cryptocurrency trading at £100. This crypto then starts to crash and we dip down to £60. On account 2 when we see that it is starting to calm and stop dipping, we can then enter let's say at £62, and then we can start profiting from this account whilst we wait for the price to get back up to £100 and then get into profit on account 1.

My biggest loss to date however has not been through liquidation. I had learnt my lesson through my previous liquidation and now used stop losses on all my orders so that if the market turned, I could stop the trade at a loss before it hit my liquidation level and took my entire margin position.

Stop losses are great but they can still mean you can take a hit, and this time I took a large one. Eye-wateringly large in fact (well, by my standards), to the tune of £5,000. Ouch I hear you cry! Yes, I know, it was traumatic, and it happened at the start of a new bull run in July 2020. Following the start of the coronavirus pandemic in early 2020, the economic and financial markets had fluctuated massively. The stock markets were crashing, people were losing their jobs and I was confident at the time that crypto would follow this trend and crash too. So, I entered a short position and held it for about three weeks, waiting for this big drop that I thought was going to happen. Then, suddenly, the market started to move up and up, and then up some more. Both Bitcoin and Ethereum blew through previous resistance levels and kept on going, signalling the start of a bull run. There was no way I could save my short position any more than I had, my leverage was as low as I could go but I knew I would get liquidated if I didn't cut the position myself. I entered a stop loss, meaning that when it hit a certain figure it would close the position, and at the end of July I couldn't fight the inevitable anymore. My short position closed, bringing my total balance from just shy of £8000 back down to under £3000. It was a big punch to the gut. It was also a classic illustration of how you can trade on the market moving up *or* down. You might be reading this thinking how can it be that if the market for Bitcoin and Ethereum was defying expectations and surging upwards that you traded in them and were now facing your worst *loss*. Surely, gains are a good thing?? It would have been an amazing profit if I had entered a long trade and bet it would go up. Unfortunately, as I thought it would go down, I made a massive loss.

The key phrase here is 'defying expectations.' I had entered some trades on the expectation that the market would move downwards following the huge disruption triggered by the start of the global pandemic. All the trends I was seeing pointed to a continuation of the initial slump in prices that I had been tracking. What has in fact happened since early 2020, certainly up to spring 2021 is that, as a deeper trend, crypto has begun to be regarded more widely as a safer, more mainstream financial asset in the face of massive global uncertainty. I will talk more about this in the final chapter of this book.

Anyway, in July 2020, I didn't read the market in that way, and suffered the consequences. I remember feeling that shame again and when I told my partner and my parents. I can still see their reaction vividly: they all kind of just gasped at me. I don't know if they were wondering why I wasn't in floods of tears, but even though I felt sad, I also felt weirdly empowered. Almost like it happened so that I could wipe the slate clean and build things up again. I felt excited, as it meant I could now take advantage of this new bull run which was an event and trading pattern I had not seen before and has proven to be unprecedented.

The thing was, it worked. That first week of August I made nearly £1,000 back and was confident the rest would follow soon after. I just had to learn the lessons, build on what I had researched, and restructure my game plan. I began setting myself daily and weekly goals. I currently have four accounts which I trade on and I have broken each down into a basic, easy format so that, at any point, I know how many trades I need to enter on each account to earn a certain amount. Now that I have this far more structured, systematic set-up in place I know I have placed myself in a far stronger position to relaunch my push to make one million. And thankfully, since adopting this new approach, I have now recovered all my losses and have learnt valuable lessons to stop them from ever being as bad again!

The key things to take away from this chapter are:

- To protect your trades, do not trade with large margin positions or a large leverage.

- Ensure that your liquidations are as far away as possible.
- It is always best to have a stop loss in place than to let yourself get liquidated; however, sometimes this isn't always possible. For example, if you have a trade set to limit order overnight and it hits whilst you are asleep, your trade could move quickly the other way and you could be liquidated even before you wake up the next morning. This should be unusual, as limit orders whilst you sleep should be on super low leverage. However, scam wicks can always happen and catch you out, so that is the risk you take with overnight trades.
- If you do get liquidated or even stopped out, take a break! Go for a walk, have some downtime away from your screen and re-group your emotions and your head space!

The moral of the story, when it comes to liquidation, is that sometimes you need it to happen to make you realise you aren't invincible. I now believe I am a better trader because of my losses. I'm not saying you need to go through the baptism of losing five grand before you become an effective crypto trader, just that some sort of loss does sharpen your focus. Hopefully this book will help you to avoid a five-grand moment, but I wouldn't be giving you the whole picture if I didn't make you aware of how easily it can happen. So, always trade with the mindset that you need to protect your portfolio, this is why stop losses exist, so use them wisely!

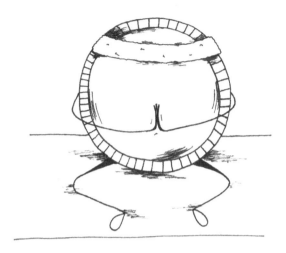

CHAPTER 11:

Patience and Practice

One of the most important tactics and strategies to have with trading is patience. You could be the most financially astute, in tune and self-aware human being there is but if you don't have patience, then crypto trading is not for you. Dale Gillham is one of Australia's most respected stock market analysts and whilst cryptocurrency isn't directly correlated with the stock market, the habitual mental state required to trade stocks is exactly the same as that for cryptocurrency. Gillham believes there are three basic attributes needed by a successful trader. These are **knowledge**, **experience** and **effort**. Living by these three attributes will lead to success.

» **Acquire knowledge:** That is exactly what you are doing by reading this book! It is vital that you understand the basics of the new world you are entering and that you have the want and desire to keep on learning. Part of the fascination *is* that there is so much to learn and that you never stop acquiring new insights and information about how to trade successfully in the crypto market. I mentioned *Coin Telegraph* and *The Daily Hodl* in Chapter 8 as sources of news, and I would strongly recommend that you subscribe to one or more news sites of this type.

» **Learn from experience:** Every trade, every success and every setback is experience you need to learn from. Keep your own crypto diary, even if only in the form of brief notes, noting, at least for the first few months, the circumstances surrounding each trade, why you chose to do it, and the outcome. A series of trades and why you entered into them can all too quickly become a blur in your memory, and vital lessons learned can easily be forgotten. Once you have gained a few months' experience you can probably ease off on the level of notetaking, it's up to you. These notes can also take the form of your Excel spreadsheet that we mentioned in Chapter 4. Writing down things like where you entered and exited, your leverage and what profit you made, helps to see where you are going right, or wrong.

» **Put in the effort:** As with most things in life, to achieve success, you must commit to learning, growing, practising and putting that effort into trading or you will never reap the rewards. One of the reasons why I wanted to write this book was to show people that you do not need to be a genius or a skilled mathematician to be able to trade – all you need is the will to want to learn and the determination to reach your goals.

There is a general statistic associated with trading the stock market, but I believe applies equally to cryptocurrency. This statistic is that 90% of traders fail to make money when trading. Over time, 80% lose, 10% break even and just 10% consistently make money.

Breaking this statistic down it is easy to see why 80% of traders lose, or in a sense fail, and I believe this is largely down to mindset. If you enter trading with a gung-ho attitude, believe that you know it all and have 'making money' as your only goal, then you will not be a successful trader. Without sounding like I am preaching a hippy kind of spiritual mindset, because I'm not, I do not believe you can trade successfully without being aware of your own mental state. Entering into trading, whether it is your first or one thousandth trade, your mindset must be exactly the same. You need to be calm and strategic; you must be organised and have a checklist that you mentally follow for each and every trade.

This checklist includes knowing or finding out before you enter a trade:

— What direction is the market moving in?
— Are you entering long or short because of this market trend?
— How big is your position going to be, which means how many contracts will you be putting into that order?
— Are you going to limit or market buy in?
— What is your leverage?
— What price do you want to enter in at and what price will you exit at?

Running through this checklist either mentally or on paper is how you can work out whether a trade is worth it. Learning and understanding that not every day is a trading day is what will take you out of that 80% of losing traders. Ideally, our goal is to be part of the 10% of traders who win consistently. Now, that being said, it is virtually impossible for anyone to have a 100% win-rate and never have a trade that loses or that they have to cut so that they don't lose. The only way I could see anyone having a 100% win-rate is if they either trade with no leverage and always have super lucky entry prices or they trade on such little leverage that their liquidation is nigh on impossible to ever hit. Realistically, I think every trader will have losses; these happen more frequently when you are starting out but the idea is that, as your knowledge and experience grows, so does your success.

Tapping into this stronger success rate and being part of the 10% win rate is where I believe mindset trumps so many of the other indicators that we use to trade. This is where patience comes into the core mindset of trading and is why I feel it is so important to address and really reinforce how crucial it is to master this. Having said that, I am one of the most impatient people I know. It has taken me a long time to get to the level of restraint I have now with trading, as it is hard to separate your emotions from the trade.

It is important to learn how to compartmentalise your emotions in trading because when we trade with emotion this is when we are more likely to get liquidated or stopped out. As I say, I am the worst person for wanting to trade when I shouldn't. If I'm bored and not in a trade, then I want to get into one. If I'm excited and not in a trade I want to get into one. Basically, I now find that I always want to trade! However, it isn't always a good time to do so, and this is what I have struggled with learning and accepting. The attitude that I initially had when I began trading put me in the 80% of traders who will fail. There was no doubt that if I had continued trading how I was at the beginning I would have either given up or lost all my money by now. I had to learn to CALM DOWN! I had to teach myself not to have a constant FOMO attitude and rush into the market when it was just going up, up, up. I had to learn that what goes up must come down, and that buying a dip would be much more profitable than trying to buy in at the top of the market trend for that day. I had to force myself to learn self-restraint and I would say it probably took me about 6 months of recklessness before I truly had my trading "aha" moment.

When you first begin trading you will have made so many notes from the research you have undertaken that this can act as a misleading safety net. It makes you feel that, now you have learnt all this knowledge and can implement all this advice, there is no way that you can fail. That may even be factually correct in relation to a specific trade you are looking at. However, as humans we do not always do what is logical and we let our emotions take over. We disregard the things we know we should do and end up taking a risk. This is when things tend to go wrong. Multiple times I have thought that I knew what I was doing and that "just one more trade" at a silly price level or leverage would be fine. However, it would be that one trade outside of my logical plan which would lead to my house of cards collapsing and then I have had to start again.

Upon speaking with someone in a crypto forum I follow I was explaining that, whilst I felt I understood what I was doing, I kept making the same mistakes. I knew they were mistakes; I knew I shouldn't be entering on a high leverage with the majority of my wallet, but I was still doing it! It was as if I couldn't help myself. The desire to make money and make money quickly was sweeping me up into this bubble of awful trading decisions, and whilst I would have a few successful trades I would then do something silly and nuke myself and my wallet. I never considered myself to have an addictive personality – I don't drink and have never done drugs – and yet I was finding that I was becoming addicted to needing to trade, to get my fix, and this wasn't healthy.

It was at this point in the conversation when I received a perfect piece of advice which changed how I viewed what I was doing. My comrade said:

"Treat £100 as if it is £1 million pounds. How do you expect to consistently make money and keep it, if you can't even make £100? Stop focusing on price points, stop trying to over-analyse what could or might happen. Stop focusing on what other traders are doing. Just stop. Instead, focus on what the market is showing you. Focus on what is right in front of you and buy the dips it presents you. Protect your money, whether it is £10, £100 or £10,000. Look after it, and it will look after you."

I knew I had to make a change. I had to go slower and go back through all the research and information I had gathered if I was ever going to start trading successfully, consistently and safely.

Profit is profit

Emotions such as greed, anxiety, recklessness and even anticipation will affect how you enter and exit a trade, along with the length of time you stay in a trade. When I first began trading, one of the hardest things for me to learn was knowing when to take profit and say enough is enough. "Profit is profit" is a mantra you need to repeat to yourself whenever you are in a trade and are unsure when to exit. It is so easy to say to yourself, just one more pound or dollar movement up or down and I'll come out. But then you don't exit, just in case it keeps going and your profit increases – and, believe me, this is precisely the moment when things can and will go wrong. You can always enter another trade, there will always be money to be made tomorrow or the next day but holding onto a trade in the hope it will just go a little further is more often than not when a trade can turn on you and you end up with a loss. Timing is everything! When the market is moving up quite quickly you can use trading indicators such as a trailing stop loss to help you lock in profit before the market moves against you.

To combat emotion and to overcome the "just a little more" mindset, it is preferable that you already know how much you want the trade to move before you exit. For example, say you place a long trade thinking the trend is going to continue in an upward movement. Before you enter, you need to calculate how many contracts your position will include, at what price you want to enter the market and at what price you want to exit. Let's say you want to exit the trade after the market has moved up by £5 or $5, depending on what platform you are trading on. Knowing that this is your goal will allow you to mentally prepare for the profits of that trade and stop you saying just, just, just! Even if the market continued to move up another £10/$10, that is OK because you came out in profit and profit is profit!

It is so important to be in a relaxed and calm state of mind when reading the charts and analysing what your moves should be. Sometimes when pumps start, it can be hard not to rush in and place a trade to try and take quick advantage. I have often had trades placed at certain levels to pick up mini dips and then I see it starting to pump and think I need to cancel that trade and move my price up to get in as quickly as possible. Already, this is my clear strategy unravelling!

It is better to have, as part of a clear strategy instead of panicky reaction, the use of laddering as a systematic way to exploit pumps in the market. When the market starts to move quickly, one way to take advantage, instead of having just one entry price, is conduct laddering. There are different definitions of laddering – however in this context we are referring to buying into the market at various different price points in order to achieve one average entry price. This allows us to take advantage of dips or peaks depending on whether you are going long or short.

For example, say you wanted to go long and buy £1000 worth of a cryptocurrency, currently pricing itself around the £80-£100 mark but showing signs that it is looking to move up. Instead of just entering the trade at £100 with your 1000 contracts, you could instead enter 4 separate orders each worth 250 contracts at various price points below £100. For example, you could enter at £85, £90, £95 and £100. This would give you an average entry price of around £92.50. This is where you ladder into the trade because you are buying in at different price points.

You can also ladder out of a trade and take profits at different price points too. Whilst this is a good way to take advantage of dips or peaks and the unknown of candle wicks, it isn't a trading strategy that I would recommend for an initial starter. Once you have got the hang of just having one entry and exit price though, you can move on to laddering. The good thing about laddering is that it combines the benefits of patience with satisfying that niggling fear of missing out because it allows you to enter the market at different price points to achieve one average price. In this way you can take advantage of a fast-moving market, whilst also keeping your entry price as high or low as possible depending on whether you are long or short.

Whilst emotion in trading is completely normal, because as human beings we don't want to miss out on things, 9 times out of 10 those pumps come back down. Whilst you may have to wait another 2, 12, or 24 hours for it to happen, it will if you haven't been too ambitious with how deep you think the market will dip.

Practice trading

Now, when it comes to being successful in trading, the key thing is to have a set strategy that works for you. It is finding out what is making you money consistently in a safe and protective way, which you can then rinse and repeat multiple times over. Find your winning formula and stick to it!

The good news is that you can practise trading without spending any money! One of the platforms to practice trading with pretend Bitcoin on is BitMEX's practice platform called TestNet. This allows you to register for a pretend trading account, with a pretend deposit of Bitcoin, to practice and learn about the platform and how it works before you register for a real account using real funds.

There are other platforms that offer practice sites, including eToro and Trading View, which are my personal favourites. A quick google search will pull up various practice cryptocurrency sites, and you can then see which interface and layout you prefer.

From this chapter there are a few things you should have noted or taken away from it. These are:

- Grow your portfolio slowly.
- Do not rush and make silly mistakes by trying to grow your wallet too quickly.
- Profit is profit, regardless of how small. If you can make £1 you can make £1 million.
- Have a strategy and only trade when you are in a patient and calm mindset.
- Practice your strategy multiple times.
- Consistency is critical.

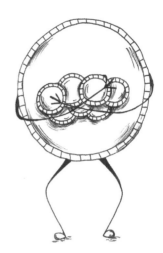

CHAPTER 12:

Hodling

We are now going to talk about holding cryptocurrency and the best and safest ways to protect and look after your money. Whilst you may think at first glance that the title of this chapter has a spelling mistake, there is a story behind it.

In 2013, a drunk contributor to a Bitcoin forum misspelled 'hold' when writing about what he was doing with his Bitcoin. At 10.03am UTC, on 18th December 2013, the contributor "GameKyuubi" wrote this exact statement:

"I AM HODLING," "I type d that tyitle twice because I knew it was wrong the first time. Still wrong. w/e, WHY AM I HOLDING? I'LL TELL YOU WHY," he continued. "It's because I'm a bad trader and I KNOW I'M A BAD TRADER. Yeah you good traders can spot the highs and the lows pit pat piffy wing wong wang just like that and make a millino bucks sure no problem bro."

This drunken spelling mistake stuck and 'To Hodl' has since become the term across the world that refers to buy-and-hold strategies in the context of Bitcoin and other cryptocurrencies. The term Hodlers describes traders who buy a cryptocurrency and then hold on to it for the long term. The typo has been turned to good use, with HODL also meaning Hold On for Dear Life.

Due to the volatility of the crypto world, I, along with many other traders, believe that holding coins is a core part of being involved with cryptocurrency. Whether you hold a portion of your investment for 1, 5 or even 10 years, investing into crypto for its long-term possibilities is a great way of passively earning an income.

When I decided to start trading, I took my initial investment, which was £1000, and split it in half. I put £500 into a trading platform and used the other £500 to buy various amounts of different cryptocurrencies to hold. I don't worry about whether the crypto I have chosen to hodl goes up or down too much as I am in it for the long haul. I know from the research that I conducted when I bought them that they are strong projects that will hopefully only go up in price over time.

As to where those cryptocurrencies should be held and safely stored, it is a personal preference. However, there are a few options that vary in security level which you should take into account when making your holding decisions.

A cryptocurrency wallet

A cryptocurrency wallet is a software program that stores private and public keys. It can take the form of a device, an online program or even be a paper document. These 'keys' are part of an encryption scheme that are mathematically related, but not identical. The private key is used to decrypt your wallet and the public key is used to encrypt it. Your public key can be shared whereas the private key is secret, which ensures that only the owner can decrypt the content.

The combination of these keys interacts with various blockchains to enable users to send and receive digital currency and to monitor their balance. In layman's terms, a cryptocurrency wallet is what can hold your cryptocurrency. Each coin has its own personal 'address' which is what you use when you deposit and withdraw that cryptocurrency from the wallet.

The most secure way of holding and storing your cryptocurrency is through something called a hard wallet; this is also referred to as a cold storage wallet.

A hard/cold storage wallet

A hard wallet is a physical device, similar to a USB stick, which can hold cryptocurrency. There are two main leaders within the hard wallet market: Trezor and Ledger. I recommend purchasing these devices directly through their website or through their listed stockists. These devices are security sealed to ensure authenticity and will also self-verify themselves with the company when you set them up. Both have different price points because they each support different cryptocurrencies. The type of coins you wish to purchase and invest in will affect which wallet is most suitable. I would recommend researching both to see which you prefer.

These devices are completely secure and limit your risk and exposure to hackers and cryptocurrency theft. When setting up a hard wallet you will need to create special passwords, called seeds, and the suppliers will also supply you with information that only relates to that device. It is critical you keep all this information safe because if you lose your recovery seeds, passwords and information, you will lose access forever to that device and the coin stored on it.

Think of your hard wallet like your own personal bank. The device is only connected to the internet when you plug it in to access the coins stored on it. When it is not plugged into your device it is completely safe and your crypto is protected. You may have seen news reports about people being locked out of their Bitcoin or losing their devices and therefore losing access to their money. These stories are true and reinforce the importance of looking after your hard wallet. Think of it in terms of our typical banking system – if you had a large amount of money in a bank account but lost your identity and all your ID paperwork, they wouldn't let you take the money out. The same thing applies to your hard wallet – if you lose the device or you lose the access codes to it then you are locked out forever.

The main reason that this is often referred to as a cold storage wallet is because it is stored away from the internet. The cryptocurrency's private keys are stored in an offline environment on the physical device, which protects them from online attacks.

Online/hot storage wallets

Hot storage wallets are digital wallets that store your cryptocurrency online in some form. There are multiple different platforms that you can use for digital storage; however, it needs to be noted that storing your cryptocurrency online is not as secure as it being in an offline format.

A desktop wallet is a type of wallet that can be downloaded onto your personal computer. This will only be accessible from the computer that it was downloaded onto and it does offer a high level of security. However, if your computer got infected with a virus or was hacked then you could lose your money.

A mobile wallet is similar to a desktop wallet but is simplified for ease of use on a mobile. It is downloaded as an application (app) and will then be accessed by a secure password and set-up that you will create upon downloading the app. Both the desktop and the mobile wallet, whilst technically storing the crypto on your device, are still connected to the internet and are therefore not 100% secure.

An online wallet runs on the cloud and there are multiple online wallets. I do not personally recommend using this to store your cryptocurrencies long term as your keys are held online and are controlled by a third party which means they are extremely vulnerable to hacking attacks and theft.

Exchange wallets

There are some types of online wallets whereby you log into an online platform to access your crypto. Some exchanges like Binance allow you to leverage trade and also spot buy and sell cryptocurrency. You can then keep that coin on their platform for however long you want.

A few examples of other online wallets on exchanges are:

- Coinbase
- Crypto.com
- Kraken

Whilst these are great platforms to buy cryptocurrency and even stake that coin for the short term, for long-term holding it is better to keep your money safe in a cold wallet. I cannot stress enough how important it is to do your own research on which platforms you prefer and their infrastructure. Whilst the above platforms are ones I like and have used, everyone has different requirements for what they want to do with their cryptocurrency, and different IT ability. This is why you need to find an exchange and a trading platform that suits your needs best.

As previously stated, the information and opinions expressed in this book are not financial advice; I am not a financial advisor, nor am I trained within the financial world. I hope however that the content, gained from my experience and the knowledge I have gathered to date, will help guide others in the right direction.

Trading wallets

As well as having wallets in the exchanges where you can buy and sell your crypto, you can also have your wallet or portfolio of coins that you actively trade. These will be held on your chosen trading platform like BitMEX, Binance, Bittrex or ByBit.

These platforms should only hold your crypto for a short while or whilst you are trading. As your portfolio or trading wallet grows, you should get in the habit of moving your excess cryptocurrency out so that it can be stored in a safer way. For example, for every £50 of Bitcoin that you make on the trading platform, you could move out £30 of Bitcoin, back to your cold storage wallet for safekeeping.

We have previously mentioned wallet addresses and how you use these to send crypto between accounts. Your chosen holding wallet, whether that is digital or physical, will have its own unique wallet address. As always, ensure these details are kept safe.

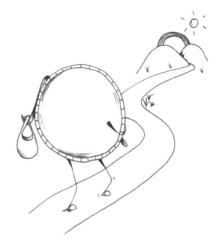

CHAPTER 13:

Your Crypto Starter Journey

Throughout this book, I have tried to create examples and illustrate the various aspects and elements of trading. However, I understand how daunting this world can be and how intense and full of jargon it is. My main goal in writing this book has been to create something that helps to break down the cryptocurrency world to enable anyone to be able to understand it on an introductory level so they can then expand on that knowledge by embarking on their own crypto journey.

As I have mentioned previously, I truly believe that education and knowledge never ends. There is always more to learn, with new skills to acquire and discovering better ways of doing things. With the evolution and constant growth of crypto, there will always be new creations, new platforms and new cryptocurrencies within this industry. Despite this constant innovation (or maybe because of it?), I understand you may still be cautious. You will have still only have fully absorbed some portions of this book and trust me, I know you will need to go back and re-read things like I did over and over until they compute. It will only be once you have opened an account and have started staring at some trading screens when many of the trading concepts will crystalise in your head.

So, if you are still unsure as to how on earth you can dip your toe in this world and are still in a mind haze, here is a step-by-step breakdown of a journey to your possible first trade.

Please remember that **this is not financial advice** and the examples below are only a suggestion based on my personal experiences and my own introduction to crypto. At the time of writing this is a sensible opening strategy, but please, as stated before, only trade and invest what you can afford to lose.

I started out with a total investment pot of £1000 and I am using this sum as an illustration here. This may sound a sizeable amount of money, but, as you will see, this is divided up into a number of different smaller pots, each traded in a different way. This is a great way to spread your risk AND a good way to acquaint yourself from the outset with different styles of trading and types of cryptocurrency. For example, straightaway I will be dividing the £1000 into two pots of £500, one to invest in long-term passive trading, and the other £500 to use for my active day trading. The day trading pot will sub-divide further, as you will see below.

Step 1 – Convert your £1000 fiat currency on your chosen exchange

As I am in the United Kingdom, my two favourite exchanges to use are crypto.com and Coinbase. If I know what cryptocurrency I would like to purchase I use crypto.com because they allow you to log on, select which cryptocurrency and how much you would like to buy, and then purchase it automatically from the credit/debit card you set up on the account.

If I don't know what crypto I yet want to buy, then I use Coinbase because they allow you to simply send your £1000 to your Coinbase account where it can then sit until you know what and how much you want to buy.

As outlined in Chapter 6, *Using an Exchange*, there are a variety of exchanges you can choose to use depending on your location. For the purposes of this example, and trying to make this step-by-step journey as easy as possible, I am going to continue on the basis that I am just using Coinbase, and I have sent my entire £1,000 to this exchange.

So, my £1,000 is now sat in my Coinbase account in the GBP section of my portfolio waiting for me to spend it. It does not cost anything to send GBP to Coinbase, as you only start paying fees on this specific exchange when you buy and sell cryptocurrency.

Step 2 – Splitting my £1,000 investment

Now my £1,000 is in my exchange account, I am going to split it in half, giving me £500 to buy cryptocurrencies that I plan on holding for a long period of time. We will call this our long-term pot, and the £500 for active day trading we will call our short-term pot. For the purposes of this example, I am going to use BitMex as my chosen day trading platform. As mentioned previously, BitMex only accept Bitcoin so I need to convert my active day trading money into Bitcoin.

I do this by purchasing £500 worth of Bitcoin on Coinbase. This is all quite straightforward when you are on the exchange as it is an easy-to-use website. Depending on the fees on that day, for a transaction of £500 I could expect to pay anything between £10-£15 for conversion from GBP to Bitcoin.

Let's say the fee was £10, so I now have £490 worth of Bitcoin in the Bitcoin section of my Coinbase portfolio and I am now ready to send that to my chosen trading platform. It is at this point I would urge you to explore the trading platform you have chosen and study their how-to instructional guides and videos, because every platform is different. If I tried to explain this process to you in written form it would make little sense, as the process of sending your Bitcoin to a trading platform differs for each one.

Step 3 – Splitting your short-term pot

At this point you have two options with your £490 worth of Bitcoin:

1. You can send the entire amount to one trading platform account to actively trade.
2. You can further split your short-term pot and distribute or send it to multiple accounts. What I mean by this is, with BitMex for example, you can create multiple email addresses and then open multiple BitMex accounts. You need to complete KYC with your ID on each account, but once done, you then have, let's say, 4 different accounts.

By splitting up your short-term pot, it gives you more trading flexibility. You can then split your short-term pot equally between all 4 accounts or however you want to. With my accounts I like to have them split as follows:

1. One account for longing. I only go long in this account.
2. One account for shorting. I only go short in this account but if my long account starts to go down, I can then counterbalance my loss on that account by going short on this one and therefore still make money whilst being stuck on the other account.
3&4. I then have 2 spare trading accounts which only have around £100 worth of Bitcoin in them and these are for emergencies. If I am stuck in my other two accounts due to large market

movements, I can still trade and conduct small trades using these two spare accounts.

Assuming you have now sent your £490 worth of Bitcoin to your trading platform, ready for active day trading, you will now be left with £500 in your Coinbase GBP section.

Step 4 – Splitting your long-term pot

Your remaining £500 can now be split between whichever cryptocurrencies you like the look of! This is a completely personal choice and I do not suggest you invest in one over another, but I personally like having a little bit in each of the key players we talked about in Chapter 3.

In my holding long-term pot, I currently have 26 different cryptos, with my largest percentages being in Bitcoin, Ethereum, Litecoin, Cardano, Polkadot, Stellar Lumens and Chainlink. Again, **this is not financial advice**, and you need to research every crypto you invest in. I do not have equal splits either, so you can split your £500 into £10 investments if you want to.

Once you have split up your long-term pot and purchased the relevant cryptocurrencies you want to hold, you can choose to leave them in Coinbase. However, as outlined earlier, this is known as a hot or online storage wallet so could still be hacked or attacked by thieves. I would therefore recommend moving your long-term cryptocurrencies to a cold storage wallet, either in the form of a Trezor or Nano wallet.

How long you choose to hold these cryptocurrencies is, again, totally up to you! Some may choose to hold for a week, a month or a year. Personally, I have made the decision to not touch anything in my cold storage wallet for at least 5 years, to see where they go.

To put into perspective how much growth potential there is with simply holding a cryptocurrency, I invested £500 into various cryptos in May 2020 and as at March 2021, my current long-term pot is sat at £8,429.28! Now that is a lot more than my bank would have given me in interest! When you look at crypto gains like this, it really makes you excited for the future and what could potentially happen!

So, that is purely an example of how you could choose to set up the structure of your own first crypto trading journey. It is one that has worked well for me, using a substantial enough opening stake that even when I sub-divided it I had some reasonably meaningful amounts of currency to trade with, but not too eye-watering an amount that if I lost it all there would be serious financial consequences.

Decide on what represents that sort of balance for you and then feel free to make a start! Following these four steps will have spread your risk and will give you a good taster of the various styles of trading and the trading platforms. If you *do* take the plunge, I hope this book serves as a useful starter guide for you.

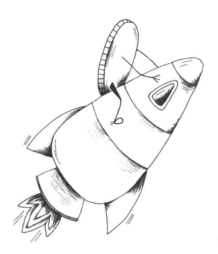

CHAPTER 14:

Welcome to the Future

I entered the crypto world as a naïve, self-conscious individual who hated maths and figures, and avoided conversations about finance at all costs. Learning about cryptocurrency and how to trade it successfully has changed not only how I see and think about myself, but also how I interact and think about my finances.

I can honestly say that learning this skill is the best thing I have ever done, and I wish someone had introduced me to this world when I was younger. I am 29 years old now and I wish I could talk to the 19-year-old me and introduce her to the wonders of investing, trading and just managing money in a better way.

The misconceptions and negativity that surround the crypto world can make it seem like an industry that should be avoided at all costs. It is undeniable that it is risky and unpredictable. Cryptocurrency is even more volatile than the stock market and it certainly is not for the faint-hearted. You will have days where your heart is in your mouth because you are in a trade and the market is going the other way. It is scary and unreliable, but it is also exhilarating, exciting and so rewarding!

Charles Hoskinson, the founder of Cardano (ADA) made a poignant statement in a YouTube interview in February 2021, which has really resonated with me and I think explains the endless possibilities and reasons as to why we should allow cryptocurrency to integrate into our society. He stated:

"The point of an inclusive system is despite the differences in your background, you should have the power somehow to rise within the system. The point of the legacy systems and why we seek to destroy them is that they don't do that. They don't have that property; they don't look at people for being people. Instead, they look at them as commodities and they value them accordingly. Many parents tell their children, make sure you study a field to make money, become a doctor, become a lawyer, become an accountant, become an engineer. It doesn't matter if that's your passion or what you're good at; go do it because it's safe and predictable. And then with that money, the limited time you have left after your stress from doing a job you hate, go spend that money somehow doing the things you like two weeks a year. And that's a good life. What kind of a system inflicts that upon people? We need to change. And the point of this industry is to change the way society works, to change the way companies work, to change the way we make decisions, to change the way property works, to change the way value works, to enable people to modify things they never thought were monetizable".

Learning to trade in a responsible way, making yourself accountable for your actions, and ensuring that you only trade when there is a clear direction, are hard rules to follow but they are critical to being successful in this world.

I have no doubt that in only a few short years, cryptocurrency will have integrated itself within our society so deeply that the misconceptions and current negativity associated with it will be a thing of the past. Of course, there will always be those who remain sceptical and do not wish to have anything to do with this world and that is okay. It isn't something that everyone will want to be a part of but, just like our fiat currency, I believe crypto will become something we use daily within our society, potentially without even realising it.

Writing this book has made me realise how much I truly love this subject and the cryptocurrency world. I hope it has helped to inspire you and provide easy-to-understand information to start your own cryptocurrency adventure!

CHAPTER 15:

Crypto Glossary

The world of crypto is full of technical terms and acronyms plus some bewildering slang and abbreviations. Here is an A-Z glossary, providing a comprehensive set of definitions for most of the commonly used terms. Many of these are mentioned in the book – so if you want to know the difference between *Bart* and *Brrr*, and discover that you don't order chop chop suey in a Chinese restaurant, then read on...

A

Algorithm

An algorithm is a process or set of rules to be followed when it comes to problem solving or calculating operations. It is usually done by a computer although certain people are able to solve complex problems algorithmically.

All Time High (ATH) and All Time Low (ATL)

The all-time high is the highest point that a cryptocurrency has been in its history. The all-time low is the lowest price point it has been in its history.

Altcoin

The term altcoin or alternative coin refers to every cryptocurrency released after Bitcoin, which was the first cryptocurrency to ever be released. Many like to sell themselves as being better than Bitcoin by trying to fix problems Bitcoin has encountered. There is an altcoin that makes faster transactions, another that is less volatile, another that is more private and so on. Altcoins play an important role by expanding the boundaries of blockchain possibilities and the scope of applications.

Anti-Money Laundering (AML)

AML is a set of international laws which have been created to try to curtail criminal organisations or individuals laundering money through cryptocurrencies into fiat.

Application Programming Interface (API)

API is a set of routines, protocols and tools for building software applications.

Arbitrage

This is the practice of taking advantage of differences in price of the same asset in two or more markets or exchanges. For example, an arbitrage trader could be in both a US market and an Australian market due to prices of a cryptocurrency varying on different exchanges.

Ask Price

This is the lowest ask order in an open market. In any financial market, buyers and sellers place their orders to determine the highest price they are willing to buy at and the lowest price at which they are willing to sell. The buyers place bids and sellers place asks, or offers to sell. If a bid is higher than an ask, a trade occurs, as the buyer is willing to pay more than the value that the seller wants.

Atomic Swap

This is a way of letting people directly exchange one type of cryptocurrency for another on a different blockchain or off-chain without a centralized intermediary such as an exchange.

B

Bag and Bagholder
A bag is a significant quantity of a specific cryptocurrency. There is no exact amount on how much is considered a bag but a bagholder is someone who is considered to hold a large amount.

Bart
When people refer to a Bart movement on the market it is when the trading chart mimics the profile of Bart Simpson's hair. By this you will see a sharp climb upwards, followed by sideways movement and then another sharp movement downwards. This up and down distribution pattern has become known in the crypto market as a Bart pattern.

Bear Market
A bear market is a situation within the digital currency market defined by caution and hesitation. During a bear market, people are more likely to sell than buy. You can expect to see lower highs and lower lows. It is a sustained period of time, characterised by downward movements.

Bear Trader
A bear trader is someone who prefers to 'short'; they want to sink the price of an asset and enjoy seeing downward trends. They buy at the tops of a price point so that they can ride the wave down.

Bear Trap
A bear trap is a technique used by a group of bullish traders to manipulate the market. They sell large amounts of cryptocurrency to trick bears into thinking the market is declining. Bearish traders sell their assets and then the bulls release the trap, allowing them to buy that asset cheaper and then make more profit when the price goes back up.

Bitcoin
Bitcoin is the first cryptocurrency to ever be created and is a decentralised peer-to-peer network, which means no single institution

or person controls it. A Bitcoin cannot be printed and only 21 million Bitcoins can ever be created.

Bitcoin ATM (BTM)

A machine from which you can withdraw Bitcoin, as you would with fiat.

Bits

A sub-unit of one bitcoin. There are 1,000,000 bits in one Bitcoin.

Black Swan Event

A black swan event refers to the possibility of an occurrence of an unexpected event. It can consist of a rare event, an extreme impact on the market or retrospective predictability.

Block

A block is a collection of transactions occurring during every time period on a blockchain.

Blockchain

A blockchain is a digital record of transactions. The name comes from its structure, in which individual records, called blocks, are linked together in a single list, called a chain. Blockchains are used for recording transactions made with cryptocurrencies, such as Bitcoin, and have many other applications.

Block Explorer

This is an online tool which allows you to view all the transactions that have taken place on the blockchain, as well as network hash rate (see hash rate definition) and transaction growth.

Block Reward

This is an incentive for miners who successfully calculate a valid hash in a block during mining.

Bots

These are automated trading software bots that execute trade orders very quickly based on a pre-set algorithm of buy and sell rules.

Brrr

This is terminology you will see on forums when price action starts to increase rapidly. It is supposed to represent the sound of money being printed.

Bubble

A bubble is a situation where market participants drive prices up above their value, which is usually followed by a steep, rapid drop in prices as the market corrects.

Bull Market

A bull market is the opposite to a bear market and is when the market trend is up. This market is full of confidence and optimism and can be seen by clear growth in the digital currency market.

Bull Trader

A bull trader is someone who prefers to 'long'; they want to push the price up, believe in upward trends and 'buy the dips' in price to accumulate more of an asset.

Buy The Dip (BTD)

When price action dips, people will tell others to 'buy the dip' in anticipation that it will soon pump.

Buy Wall

Opposite to a sell wall, a buy wall is a situation within trading where a large limit order has been placed to buy when a cryptocurrency reaches a certain value. This can be used by traders to create a certain impression in the market, preventing the asset from falling below that value, as demand will likely outstrip supply when the order executes.

C

Candlesticks
A candlestick chart is a technique used to show changes in price over time. Each candle provides 4 points of price activity information: opening, closing, highest and lowest. Also known as 'candles' for short.

Centralisation/Centralised Network
Centralisation is commonly associated and used by governments and banks. Centralised cryptocurrencies keep most of the control over your account and this remains in the hands of the third party which runs the exchange.

There are several crucial disadvantages to this approach, stemming from the fact that any central authority also plays the role of a single point of failure in the system: any malfunction at the top of the hierarchy, whether unintentional or deliberate, inevitably has a negative effect on the entire system.

Chop Chop Suey
Chop chop suey is a saying you will see on the crypto forums and refers to when the market moves quickly up and down, trapping and liquidating people. The saying refers to traders getting 'chopped' to death and you will often see messages saying, "Have a bowl of chop chop suey!"

Close
This refers to the closing price.

Coin
A coin is a cryptocurrency that can operate independently.

Coinbase
Coinbase is one of the largest cryptocurrency exchanges and is ranked among the top in the world by traffic, liquidity and trading volumes according to CoinMarketCap.com, a market research website.

Cold Storage/Cold Wallet

This is an offline storage facility for cryptocurrency and is normally a physical device like a USB, an offline computer or a paper wallet. A cold wallet is a cryptocurrency wallet that is in cold storage and is not connected to the internet.

Confirmations

A cryptocurrency transaction is only confirmed when it is included in a block on the blockchain, at which point it has one confirmation. Each additional block is another confirmation. Different exchanges require a different number of confirmations to consider a cryptocurrency transaction final.

Consensus

Consensus is achieved when all participants of the network agree on the order and content of blocks and transactions contained in those blocks.

Contract

A contract is the terminology used on trading platforms to describe the size of your trade. This can also be referred to as the size of your position. Some trading platforms differ, but in BitMex 1 contract is the equivalent of $1.

Correction

A correction is a (usually negative) reverse movement of at least 10% in a cryptocurrency or general market, to adjust for over or under valuations.

Cryptocurrency

Cryptocurrency or crypto for short, is a type of digital or virtual money. It has no physical counterpart such as a banknote or coin that can be carried around. It only exists in an electronic format.

Crypto Miner

A crypto miner is responsible for ensuring the authenticity of information and updating the blockchain with the transaction. Miners get paid for verifying transactions and are essentially the cornerstone of many cryptocurrency networks as they spend their time and computing power to solve math problems set by the network, providing a so-called "proof-of-work" for the crypto network they are working on. Miners are responsible for creating new coins or tokens through this process, as they receive rewards in that coin or tokens for successfully completing a PoW task.

Cryptocurrency Wallet

A cryptocurrency wallet is a physical device, program or a service which stores your cryptocurrency. It can take the form of a hard wallet which is like a USB; a paper wallet which is an offline mechanism; or an online wallet which can be held on an exchange or cryptocurrency application.

D

Dark Web

The dark web is a portion of internet content existing on darknets, not indexed by search engines, that can only be accessed with specific software, configurations or authorisations.

Day Trading

A day trader is a trader who buys and sells their asset on the same day. A day trade will be held from a few minutes to a few hours, but all day trades will be closed by the end of their day.

Decentralisation/Decentralised Network

Decentralisation is the process of distributing and dispersing power away from a central authority. Most financial and governmental systems which are currently in existence are centralised, meaning that there is a single highest authority in charge of managing them, such as a central bank or state apparatus. Bitcoin has been designed as a decentralised alternative to government money and therefore does not have any single point of failure, making it more resilient, efficient and democratic. Its underlying technology, the blockchain, is what allows for this decentralisation, as it offers every user an opportunity to become one of the network's many payment processors. Since Bitcoin's appearance, many other cryptocurrencies, or altcoins, have appeared, and most of the time they also use the blockchain mechanism to achieve some degree of decentralisation.

DeFi

DeFi is the abbreviation for Decentralized Finance and is an ecosystem of financial applications built upon other blockchain networks such as Ethereum. DeFi represents a movement that is focused upon creating financial services that are transparent and permissionless.

Delegated Proof of Stake (dPoS)

A consensus mechanism where users can vote for delegates producing blocks on the blockchain, with votes proportional to their stake. It aims to increase efficiency and the environmental friendliness of blockchain consensus protocols.

Depth Chart

A graph that plots the requests to buy (bids) and the requests to sell (asks) on a chart, based on limit orders. The chart shows the point at which the market is most likely to accept a transaction.

Derivative

A contract deriving its value from the performance of an underlying asset, index or interest rate.

Derivatives Market

A public market for derivatives, which are instruments such as futures contracts or options derived from other forms of cryptocurrency assets.

Digital Currency Exchange (DCE)

An exchange that allows customers to trade cryptocurrencies or digital currencies for other assets such as conventional fiat money or other digital currencies.

Distributed Network

A type of network where processing power and data are spread over the nodes without a centralized data centre or authority.

Dolphin

A dolphin is a person who owns a moderate quantity of cryptocurrency. This person does not qualify to be a whale but has evolved from being a fish/minnow.

Dominance

Also known as BTC Dominance for Bitcoin Dominance, it is an index that compares the market capitalization of Bitcoin with the overall market cap of all other cryptocurrencies in existence.

Double Spending

A situation where a sum of money is illegitimately spent more than once.

Dump/Dumping

To dump is to sell off all your coins. Dumping is the action of collective market sell-offs, which creates a downward price movement.

Dusting Attack

When a scammer sends tiny amounts of a cryptocurrency to random users' wallets, and then analyses and tracks the transactions in order to identify the specific users behind each address.

Dust Transactions

Minuscule transactions that flood and slow the network, usually deliberately created by people looking to disrupt it.

DYOR

This stands for Do Your Own Research.

E

Emission

Emission, also known as Emission Curve, Emission Rate and Emission Schedule, is the speed at which new coins are created and released.

Ether
The form of payment used in the operation of the distribution application platform Ethereum, in order to incentivize machines into executing the requested operations.

Exchange
Cryptocurrency exchanges (sometimes called digital currency exchanges) are businesses that allow customers to trade cryptocurrencies for fiat money or other cryptocurrencies.

Exchange Traded Fund (ETF)
A security that tracks a basket of assets such as stocks, bonds, and cryptocurrencies but can be traded like a single stock.

F

Fiat
Fiat currency is a national currency usually issued by a country's government or central bank, such as the Great British Pound or American Dollar.

Fiat-Pegged Cryptocurrency
Also known as pegged cryptocurrency, it is a coin, token or asset issued on a blockchain that is linked to a government or bank issued currency.

Each pegged cryptocurrency is guaranteed to have a specific cash value in reserve at all times.

Fish
A fish, or minnow, is someone who holds insignificant amounts of cryptocurrencies, often at the mercy of whales who move the market up and down.

Flippening
A situation hoped for by Ethereum fans, where the total market cap of Ethereum surpasses the total market cap of Bitcoin.

FOMO
FOMO stands for Fear Of Missing Out. This is what people feel when they see the market suddenly move dramatically and they aren't either in a trade or are in a trade going the other way. They feel they are missing out on the action. For example, say the market starts to suddenly move upwards, people can see this and think, "Quick! I need to get in on this price action now!" So I need to get in on this price action now! So they FOMO in and buy higher than they probably should, but this then causes the market to move up more until it tops out. Resisting the urge to FOMO when the market moves quickly is a key part of your trading mindset.

Fork (Blockchain)
Forks, or chain splits, create an alternate version of the blockchain, leaving two blockchains to run simultaneously. An example is Ethereum and Ethereum Classic, forked after the DAO hack.

Fork (Software)
A software fork, also known as a project fork, is when developers take the technology (source code) from one existing software project and modify it to create a new project. An example is Litecoin, which was a software fork of Bitcoin.

FUD And FUDster

FUD is an acronym that stands for Fear, Uncertainty and Doubt. It is a strategy to influence the perception of certain cryptocurrencies or the cryptocurrency market in general by spreading negative, misleading or false information. A FUDster is someone who likes to spread FUD.

Funding Fees

These are the fees you pay to keep a contract/trade open on a trading platform. The longer a trade is open the more fees you pay. Ethereum is known for having high funding fees compared to Bitcoin's which are quite low.

Futures

A futures contract is a standardized legal agreement to buy or sell a particular commodity or asset at a predetermined price at a specified time in the future.

G

Gains

Gains refer to an increase in value or profit.

Gas

A term used on the Ethereum platform that refers to a unit of measuring the computational effort of conducting transactions or smart contracts, or to launch DApps in the Ethereum network. It is the fuel of the Ethereum network.

Gas Limit

A term used on the Ethereum platform that refers to the maximum amount of gas the user is willing to spend on a transaction.

Gas Price

A term used on the Ethereum platform that refers to the price you are willing to pay for a transaction. Setting a higher gas price will incentivize miners to prioritize that transaction over others.

Genesis Block

The first block of data that is processed and validated to form a new blockchain, often referred to as block 0 or block 1.

Green Trading Day

This is a day when most of the candlesticks are green, and the market trend is moving upward.

H

Hacking

Hacking is the process of using a computer to manipulate another computer or computer system in an unauthorized manner.

Halving

An event in which the total rewarded bitcoin per confirmed block halves, happening every 210,000 blocks mined.

Hard Cap

The maximum amount that an ICO will raise. If a hard cap is reached, no more funds will be collected.

Hash and Hash Function

A hash is created using an algorithm and is essential to blockchain management. A hash is a function that converts an input of letters and numbers and turns them into an encrypted output of a specific, fixed length. This output is random and no data can be recovered from it without using something called a cipher. A cipher is an algorithm used to encrypt or decrypt data.

An important property of a hash is that the output of hashing a particular document will always be the same when using the same algorithm. A hash function is any function used to map data of arbitrary size to data of a fixed size. Understanding hashing is not needed to begin trading and is a more complex side of the logistical side of the blockchain. However, it is a word you may come across which is why it is included in this glossary.

Hash Power/Hash Rate
A unit of measurement for the amount of computing power being consumed by the network to continuously operate. The Hash Rate of a computer may be measured in kH/s, MH/s, GH/s, TH/s, PH/s or EH/s depending on the hashes per second being produced.

HODL
A type of passive investment strategy where you hold an investment for a long period of time, regardless of any changes in the price or markets. The term first became famous due to a typo of 'hold' made in a Bitcoin forum, and the term is now commonly expanded to stand for Hold On for Dear Life.

Hot Storage and Hot Wallet
Hot storage is the online storage of private keys, allowing for quicker access to cryptocurrencies. A hot wallet is a cryptocurrency wallet that is connected to the internet for hot storage of crypto assets, as opposed to an offline, cold wallet with cold storage.

I

ICO (Initial Coin Offering)
An ICO or initial coin/currency offering is a type of funding that uses cryptocurrencies. It is a form of crowdfunding; however, both private and public funded ICOs exist. In an ICO, a certain amount of cryptocurrency is sold in the form or tokens or coins. These are then

promoted as future functional units of currency when or if the ICO's funding goal is met and the project launches successfully.

Index Price
The Index Price is the average price of an asset according to major spot markets and their relative trading volume.

Inflation
A general increase in prices and fall in the purchasing value of money.

Initial Bounty Offering (IBO)
An initial bounty offering, or IBO, is the limited-time process by which a new cryptocurrency is made public and distributed to people who invest time and skill into earning rewards in the new cryptocurrency, such as doing translation or marketing. Unlike an initial coin offering where you can buy coins, an IBO requires more mental commitment from the receiver.

Initial Exchange Offering (IEO)
An initial exchange offering, or IEO, refers to a fundraising event where a cryptocurrency exchange raises money on its own platform, as opposed to an ICO, where a team conducts the fundraising.

Initial Token Offering (ITO)
Similar to ICOs, but the focus with an ITO is on the offering of tokens with proven (or unproven) intrinsic utility in the form of software or usage in an ecosystem.

Instamine
A period in time, shortly after launch, when a large portion of total mineable coins or tokens are mined in a compressed time frame and then may be unevenly and quickly distributed to investors.

Intermediary/Middleman
An intermediary, or middleman, is a person or entity that acts as the go-between for different parties to bring about agreements or carry out directives.

K

Kangaroo Market
A kangaroo market is a relatively new description for a market trend that sees the market move up and down over a certain period of time without any strong uptrend or downtrend.

KYC – Know Your Customer
KYC is the process of verifying the identity of a customer to ensure that the person opening the new account is who they claim to be.

L

Lambo
Shorthand for Lamborghini, an exotic car that people often refer to in their excitement over getting rich from cryptocurrencies. You will often see this in forums when traders ask when prices may rise again by saying: "When Lambo?" It is usually combined with "When moon?"

Last Price
The last price is the last traded price for that particular asset; it differs from the market price which is the price now.

Ledger
A record of financial transactions that cannot be changed, only appended with new transactions.

Leverage
Leverage, also referred to as margin trading, is a loan offered by a broker on an exchange during trading to increase the availability of funds in trades.

Lightning Network

The Lightning Network is a second layer payment protocol that operates on top of a blockchain. Theoretically, it will enable fast, scalable transactions between and across participating nodes, and has been touted as a solution to the Bitcoin scalability problem.

Limit Order/Limit Buy/Limit Sell

Refers to orders placed by traders to buy or sell a cryptocurrency when a certain price is reached. This is in contrast to market orders where a cryptocurrency is sold at the current best available price.

Liquidation

This is something you don't want to happen, but it probably will at some point! Liquidation is when you are in a trade and it goes the opposite way to what you expected, and you end up losing your balance staked for that trade and the margin you were trading with if using leverage.

Liquidity

How easily a cryptocurrency can be bought and sold without impacting the overall market price.

Long Trade

A 'long' trade is where you buy a cryptocurrency at a certain price with the expectation that this will increase. For example: If you bought 1 whole Bitcoin at £5,000 and the price then rises to £8,000, you still own 1 Bitcoin but you have now made £3,000. Longing is when you 'bet' on the price going up.

M

Mainnet

An independent blockchain running its own network with its own technology and protocol. This is a live blockchain where its own cryptocurrencies or tokens are in use, as compared to a testnet or projects running on top of other popular networks such as Ethereum.

Margin Trading

A practice where a trader can leverage their existing funds as collateral for a loan from a broker to increase their buying power. Leveraged trades are highly risky since they can both increase your success and deepen your losses. Also known as leverage trading.

Market

An area or arena, online or offline, in which commercial dealings are conducted. Usually referred to as the crypto market, which refers to the cumulative cryptocurrencies and projects operating within the industry.

Market Capitalization/Market Cap/MCAP

Total capitalization of a cryptocurrency's price, showing its total value. It is one of the ways to rank the relative size of a cryptocurrency.

Market Order/Market Buy/Market Sell

A purchase or sale of a cryptocurrency on an exchange at the current best available price. Market orders are filled as buyers and sellers are willing to trade. This is in contrast with limit orders in which a cryptocurrency is sold only at a specified price.

Market Price

The market price is the current price at which an asset can be bought or sold.

Max Supply

The best approximation of the maximum quantity of coins that will ever exist in the lifetime of that cryptocurrency.

Mineable

Some cryptocurrencies have a system through which miners can be rewarded with newly created cryptocurrencies for creating blocks by contributing their hash power. Cryptocurrencies with this ability to generate new cryptocurrencies through the process of confirmation are said to be mineable.

Mining

Cryptocurrency mining, or crypto mining, is a process in which transactions for various forms of cryptocurrency are verified and added to the blockchain. Also known as cryptocoin mining and altcoin mining. Cryptocurrency mining has increased both as a topic and activity as cryptocurrency usage itself has grown exponentially in the last few years. Each time a cryptocurrency transaction is made, a crypto miner is responsible for ensuring the authenticity of information and updating the blockchain with the transaction.

Mining Pool

A setup where multiple miners combine their computing power to gain economies of scale and competitiveness in finding the next block on a blockchain. Rewards are split according to different agreements, depending on the mining pool. Another term for this is Group Mining.

Mining Rig

A computer being used for mining. A mining rig could be a dedicated piece of hardware for mining, or a computer with spare capacity that can be used for other tasks, only mining part time.

Mnemonic Phrase

A mnemonic phrase (also known as mnemonic seed, or seed phrase) is a list of words used in sequence to access or restore your cryptocurrency assets. It should be kept secret from everyone else. It is a standard in most Cold/Hard storage wallets.

Momentum Trading

Momentum trading occurs when a trader notices a particular asset is "breaking out". This could either be up or down, depending on how the trader likes to trend trade, but when it breaks out the trader jumps in to ride it up or down.

Money Transmitter/Money Transfer License

In the legal code of the United States, a money transmitter or money transfer service is a business entity that provides money transfer services or payment instruments, whether it is real currency, cryptocurrency or any other value. Money transmitters in the US are part of a larger group of entities called money service businesses or MSBs.

Moon

When there is a drastic upward movement in the market, traders shout "Moon" in all the forums. You will also see this represented by rocket ship emojis.

Moving Average Convergence Divergence (MACD)

A technical analysis method, it is a trend-following momentum indicator that shows the relationship between two price moving averages. The calculation is done by subtracting the 26-day exponential moving average (EMA) from the 12-day EMA.

N

Network

A network refers to all nodes in the operation of a blockchain at any given moment in time.

No Coiner

A no coiner is someone who owns no cryptocurrency and believes that crypto will fail.

Node

A node is a computer in a blockchain network that receives and relays information.

O

Offline/Online Storage

Offline storage is the act of storing cryptocurrencies in devices or systems not connected to the internet. Online storage is the act of storing cryptocurrencies in devices or systems connected to the internet, which offers more convenience but also increased risk of theft and hacking.

Open Source

Open source software is a type of software released under a license in which the copyright holder grants users the rights to study, change, and distribute the software to anyone and for any purpose. It is also a philosophy, with participants believing in the free and open sharing of information in pursuit of the greater common good.

Open/Close

The price at which a cryptocurrency opens at a given moment in time, for example at the start of the day.

Option

A contract giving the buyer the right, but not the obligation, to buy or sell an underlying asset or instrument at a specified strike price. There are American and European options, the former of which may be exercised at any time before expiration, and the latter exercised only at the expiration date.

Options Market

A public market for options, giving the buyer an option to buy or sell a cryptocurrency at a specific strike price, on or before a specific date.

Over The Counter (OTC)

Over the counter is defined as a transaction made outside of an exchange, often peer-to-peer through private trades. In jurisdictions where exchanges are disallowed or where amounts traded will move the markets, traders will go through the OTC route. OTC stocks are currently, at the time of writing, still allowed in the UK. However, like with anything, this can change with ever-changing regulation.

P

Pair
This is how we describe the trade between one cryptocurrency and another – for example the trading pair BTC/ETH (Bitcoin and Ethereum).

Paper Wallet
This is a physical document which contains your private key or seed information.

Peer-to-Peer (P2P)
In a worldwide digital peer-to-peer network, each user is (in theory) an equivalent owner and contributor of the network. Peer-to-peer networking with cryptocurrency is the exchange or sharing of information, data, or assets between parties without the involvement of a central authority. Peer-to-peer, or P2P, takes a decentralised approach to interactions between individuals and groups.

Permabear
A permabear only trades 'short' positions and does not 'long' the market and is therefore the opposite of a permabull.

Permabull
A permabull is a trader who is permanently bullish and only trades upward market movements. They will not switch to a 'short' position even if the market is in a downward trend and is therefore the opposite of a permabear.

Perpetual Contract/Trading
A perpetual contract is a special type of futures contract, but unlike the traditional form of futures, it does not have an expiry date, so you can hold a position for as long as you like. Perpetual contracts are often traded at a price that is equal or similar to spot markets.

Phishing

Phishing is when a scammer pretends to be a trusted institution or person to trick people into revealing sensitive information about themselves, which then allows them to access their bank account etc.

Ponzi Scheme

A Ponzi scheme is a fraudulent investment which involves the payment of purported returns to existing investors from funds contributed by new investors.

Portfolio

Your portfolio is the total collection of cryptocurrencies or crypto assets that you own.

Position Trading

Position traders, also known as long-term traders, are people who stay in a trade for weeks or months. They are not concerned about short-term price fluctuations because they believe their investment will be profitable in the long term.

Profit and Loss – Realised & Unrealised PNL (P&L)

On trading platforms, you will see something called Unrealised PNL and Realised PNL or P&L. The PNL part stands for Profit and Loss. Unrealised PNL is the current profit or loss of the trade or position that you have open i.e. the profit or loss that would be achieved or realised if that trade were closed immediately. The Realised PNL is your total profit or loss after the trade has been closed and fees deducted.

Proof of Work (PoW)

Proof of work is a computer protocol that has the main goal of deterring cyber-attacks. Proof of work is a requirement to define an expensive computer calculation, also called mining, that needs to be performed to create a new group of transactions on the blockchain.

Proof of Stake (PoS)

Proof of stake will make the consensus mechanism completely virtual. While the overall process remains the same as proof of work, the method of reaching the end goal is entirely different. In PoW, the miners solve cryptographically hard puzzles by using their computer resources. In PoS, instead of miners, there are validators. The validators lock up some of their crypto as a stake in the ecosystem. Following that, the validators bet on the blocks that they feel will be added next to the chain. When the block gets added, the validators receive a block reward in proportion to their stake.

Private Key

A private key, also known as a secret key, is a piece of code generated in asymmetric-key process. It is paired with a public key to be used in the decrypting of information hashed with the public key.

Public Address

This is a public address which allows the user to use it as an address to request payment.

Public Blockchain

This is a blockchain that can be accessed by anyone.

Pump and Dump

A pump and dump scheme is a type of fraud in which offenders accumulate an asset over a period of time and then artificially inflate the price before selling off what they bought to unsuspecting buyers at a higher price. Pumps and dumps tend to happen when a cryptocurrency reaches its all-time high price points or the top of its resistance levels.

Q

QR Code

A QR code is a machine-readable label that shows encoded information in a black and white graphical pattern. It is used within cryptocurrencies to share wallet addresses.

R

Red Trading Day

A red trading day is when the majority of candlesticks are red and the market trend is moving down.

REKT

The term REKT is slang terminology that you will find on crypto forums and conversation boxes within the exchanges. It is short for wrecked and means you have lost your trade either through being stopped out or being liquidated; either way you do not want to be REKT.

Relative Strength Index (RSI)

RSI is a form of technical analysis that serves as a momentum oscillator. This means that it measures the speed and change of price movements. It moves between 0 and 100. When cryptocurrency is overbought the indicator tends to be above 70. When it is considered oversold it is below 30.

Resistance Level

The resistance, or resistance level, is the price at which the price of an asset meets pressure on its way up by the emergence of a growing number of sellers who wish to sell at that price.

Return On Investment (ROI)

This is the ratio between the net profit and the cost of investing.

S

Satoshi (SATS)

Satoshi is the smallest unit of Bitcoin, with a value of 0.00000001. In trading the aim is to accumulate as many satoshis as you can. You will often see people on forums talking about "stacking those sats."

Satoshi Nakamoto

The individual or group which created Bitcoin. To this day no one knows the true identity of Satoshi Nakamoto.

Scalp Trading

Scalping involves being in and out of a trade really quickly, to take advantage of small price actions. It is most common to scalp trade on the 1-minute or 3-minute chart, taking profits within seconds or minutes. Scalp trading can be fun, as you take profits quickly. However, it is not a skill for beginners, as you need to fully understand your charts and the price movements for that crypto asset.

Scam

A scam is a fraudulent or deceptive cryptocurrency, person, service or website.

Scam Wicks

A scam wick shows a flash movement in the market, when individuals intentionally trade at a price far out of the current trading range to trigger people's stop losses, and so cause a flood of buy/sells that push the price in the direction they want it to move. These scam wicks can go up or down, and whilst they can help to pick up limit orders that are placed low, they are brutal for people who are over leveraged as it will quickly stop them out or liquidate them. (see Stop Hunt).

Scrypt

Scrypt is an algorithm used in some proof-of-work cryptocurrencies, like Litecoin. The algorithm was designed to be computationally harder to mine by requiring large amounts of memory. This means only computers that have large memory power are able to participate in this type of mining.

Secure Asset Fund for Users or #safu

After Binance was hacked, it created a secure asset fund for users which acts as an emergency insurance fund to protect the future interests of all users. After their hack, their founder tweeted that all funds were #safu. This term is now adopted and used within forums when an asset moves up or down quickly – traders will refer to their trade as being #safu if they believe they are safe from liquidation. The term can be used sarcastically by traders though, for example if the market starts to rapidly increase, bulls may taunt bears by saying "shorts are #safu" because obviously at that point they are not.

Sell Wall
A sell wall is a situation within trading where a large limit order has been placed to sell when a cryptocurrency reaches a certain value. This can be used by traders to create a certain impression in the market, preventing the asset from rising above that value, as supply will likely outstrip demand when the order executes.

Short Trade
A 'short' trade is where you expect a downward trend market to make profits from the price of your crypto going down. It allows you to borrow an asset to sell at its current price, and once the price drops you re-purchase the asset to return to the lender, making the difference as profit. For example: You make a sell order for 1 whole Bitcoin at £5,000 and the price then drops to £4,500. You can then buy back in 1 whole Bitcoin at £4,500 and have made a £500 profit from the difference.

Silk Road
The silk road was an online black market that existed on the dark web. It accepted Bitcoins for transactions – however it has now been shut down by the FBI.

Smart Contract
A smart contract is a self-executing contract with the terms of the agreement between buyer and seller being directly written into lines of code. The code and the agreements contained therein exist across a distributed, decentralized blockchain network.

Snake In The Grass
Snake in the grass is a term often seen in crypto forums and refers to a trader who waits for the perfect time to enter a trade on a clear

directional trend movement. They don't chase the price up or down but just wait for it to be optimum for them.

Soft Cap
The soft cap is the minimum amount that an initial coin offering (ICO) wants or needs to raise in order to launch. If the ICO is unable to raise the soft cap amount, the project may be called off completely.

Spot Buying
Spot buying or spot trading is when a crypto asset is purchased "on the spot" and paid for at that exact time. Spot buying is buying at one price and the spot selling is selling at another.

Spread
In trading, the spread refers to the difference between the lowest ask price and the highest bid price.

Stablecoin
A stablecoin is a new class of cryptocurrencies that attempts to offer price stability and is backed by a reserve asset. Stablecoins have gained traction, as they attempt to offer the best of both worlds—the instant processing and security or privacy of payments of cryptocurrencies, and the volatility-free stable valuations of fiat currencies.

Staking
Staking is participation in a proof-of-stake system (PoS) that allows you to put your tokens in to serve as a validator to the blockchain, and in turn you receive rewards. In Chapter 6 we look at staking and the benefits it offers to traders for making your crypto work for you!

Stop Hunt
A stop hunt refers to a chaotic period of price action. Stop hunting is the trading strategy typically initiated by larger players (Whales) who have the necessary capital to buy or sell a large amount of asset very quickly and so push the price in a certain direction to trigger the stop loss orders of other traders in the market. Stop hunting is especially powerful in leveraged markets where loan capital is traded.

Swing Trading

Swing trading is a someone who trades on a slightly longer time frame than a scalper and often has a trade open for one to seven days. They take advantage of a short-term trend and either ride the wave up or down depending on their preference. This style of trading is less intensive because it allows someone to trade part-time. As a beginner, swing trading is one of the best trading techniques to use, as it takes a lot of the pressure off you watching the screen and can help you separate your emotions.

Support Level

Opposite to a resistance level, a support level is the level at which buyers tend to purchase or enter a trade. Once a support level has been created it is rare for that asset to fall below that level.

T

Technical Analysis or TA

Technical analysis is a trading discipline used every day by stock market traders to evaluate investments and identify trading opportunities in price trends and patterns seen on charts.

Testnet

This is an alternative blockchain used by developers for testing. It is also what is referred to the program people use when practising to trade pretend Bitcoin/fiat.

Think Long Term (TLT)

You may see this in forums, and it refers to having a specific mindset where you have a longer term investment plan or strategy.

Token

A token is a digital unit that provides access and use of a larger crypto economic system. Tokens do not have a value of their own but are made so that software can be developed around them.

Tokenize

This is the process by which real world assets are turned into something of a digital value called a token.

Total Supply

This is the total amount of cryptocurrency coins in existence right now minus any coins that have been verifiably burned and destroyed.

Trader

A trader is an individual who engages in the buying and selling of financial assets in any financial market, either for himself or on behalf of another person or institution. The main difference between a trader and an investor is the duration for which they hold the asset.

Trade Volume

The amount of cryptocurrency that has been traded in the last 24 hours.

Transaction or TX

This is the act of exchanging cryptocurrencies on a blockchain.

Transaction Fee

This is the term for when a payment is made using the blockchain to transact. You will pay a transaction fee when purchasing cryptocurrency and when sending it between wallets and exchanges.

Trigger Price

The trigger price is the price at which an exchange or trading platform will sell or buy an order. When your chosen price is hit by the market it will trigger and the order will execute.

Two Factor Authentication

Two Factor Authentication or 2FA, is a security feature that demands users provide two separate verification elements to access their online account or system. This normally takes the form of a password and then a specific numerical code sent to a separate authentication application.

V

Volatility
This is when there are large variances in price and market movement. When the market becomes volatile you can expect large gains and drops, sometimes within minutes of each other.

Volume
Also referred to as market volume, this is the amount of cryptocurrency that has been traded during a certain period of time. Volume can show the direction or trend for that day on that crypto asset and can be used as a tool for indicating future prices and demand.

Virtual Private Network (VPN)
A VPN is used to secure a connection between you and the internet. Via the VPN, all your data is routed through an encrypted virtual tunnel. This disguises your IP and makes your internet location invisible to everyone. A VPN connection is also secure against external attacks and it is recommended that you invest in one if you are serious about crypto trading. They are perfectly legal to use; however, you should not use a VPN to carry out illegal activity.

W

Wash Trade
Wash trading is a form of market manipulation where traders create artificial activity in the marketplace by buying and selling cryptocurrencies simultaneously.

Weak Hands
This term describes an investor or trader who is prone to panic selling at the first sign of the market price declining.

Whale

A whale is someone who holds large amounts of cryptocurrency. As a result, they can cause carnage with their trading due to the enormity of their wealth. They can rock the market through their trades, so it is important to pay attention to certain whales and their trades. There are various platforms such as Twitter as well as forums that document what whales are up to.

White Swan Event

Opposite to a Black Swan event, a White Swan event is based on analysis which is more predictable and intuitive.

Whitepaper

A whitepaper is an official document usually issued by new blockchain projects before their ICO is released. It informs the reader about the technology, methodology, product or service being launched.

Y

Year To Date (YTD)

Year to date (YTD) refers to the period of time from the beginning of the first day of the current calendar year or fiscal year up to the current date. YTD information is useful for analysing trends over time.

Acknowledgements

I would like to thank you for purchasing this book and wanting to learn more about this wonderful new world! I hope it helps to introduce cryptocurrency in an uncomplicated way and that you learn something you didn't know before.

I would also like to thank my family, for always supporting my crazy endeavours and never doubting my ability to write this book or get involved in cryptocurrency. Thank you for always trusting me, being there for me and helping me build my dreams.

Thank you to my friends who have allowed me to try to explain what crypto is to them, even when they haven't a clue what I'm on about! I appreciate you listening and encouraging me regardless.

Finally, I would like to thank the situation I was placed in that was beyond my control. Without ordered national lockdowns, I would never have found the time to follow this interest. Not being allowed to do my 'day job' has given me the freedom and time to listen, learn, read and improve my life momentously. I know that Covid-19 has had a disastrous impact on our entire world; if I can take something positive from those events it is the opportunity its effect has given me to become a trader and crypto fanatic.

If you take only one thing away from this book, I hope it is that you can achieve anything you put your mind to. Self-belief is the first step in achieving your wildest dreams.

Thank you to you all.
Holly

Lightning Source UK Ltd.
Milton Keynes UK
UKHW021447021121
393256UK00009B/2193

9 781838 492502